Haunted by Parents

Haunted by
Parents

LEONARD SHENGOLD, M.D.

Yale University Press   New Haven and London

All my chapters were completed before somewhat different and shortened versions of a few of them were published in the following journals: portions of chapters 2, 3, and 4 appeared in *Psychoanalytic Quarterly* 71: 699–724, 2002; chapter 5 in a shortened and slightly different version appeared in *American Poetry Review* 23: 27–29, 2004; chapter 9 in a shortened and slightly different version appeared in *Psychoanalytic Quarterly* 73: 717–86; chapter 15 appeared in a shorter version in *Scandinavian Psychoanalytic Review* 27: 87–93, 2004.

The poem by Leonard Woolf reproduced in chapter 9 is from *Love Letters: Leonard Woolf and Trekkie Ritchie Parsons 1941-1968*, edited by Judith Adamson, published by Chatto and Windus. Reprinted by permission of The Random House Group Ltd.

Printed in the United States of America.

Library of Congress Cataloging-in-Publication Data
Shengold, Leonard.
Haunted by parents / Leonard Shengold.
p. ; cm.
Includes bibliographical references and index.
ISBN-13: 978-0-300-11610-6 (alk. paper)
ISBN-10: 0-300-11610-1 (alk. paper)
1. Client-centered psychotherapy. 2. Motivation (Psychology)
3. Attitude change. 4. Psychotherapy—Miscellanea. I. Title.
[DNLM: 1. Psychoanalytic Theory. 2. Medicine in Literature.
3. Parent-Child Relations. 4. Psychoanalytic Interpretation.
WM 460 S546ha 2006]
RC465.S54 2006
616.89'14—dc22   2006017551

A catalogue record for this book is available from the British Library.
The paper in this book meets the guidelines for permanence and durability of the Committee on Production Guidelines for Book Longevity of the Council on Library Resources.
10 9 8 7 6 5 4 3 2 1

Growing old means running a gauntlet of deaths of beloved relatives and friends. This book about change and loss is dedicated to my dear departed friends and "brothers": Eddie, Vann, Larry and Bill; and to their wives, my dear friends and "sisters": Jenny, Joyce, Phyllis, and Chanie.

"Que sçais-je?" (What do I know?).
—MICHEL DE MONTAIGNE, *Essays*, Book II (1580)

"Nessun maggiore dolore che ricordarsi del tempo felice nella miseria" (There is no greater sorrow than to remember a time of happiness in the midst of misery).
—DANTE, *Inferno* (1300?)

The past is our mortal mother, no dead thing. Our future constantly reflects her to the soul. Nor is it ever the new man of today [that] grasps his fortune, good or ill. We are pushed to it by the hundreds of days we have buried, eager ghosts.
—GEORGE MEREDITH, *Harry Richmond* (1871)

Why did Hamlet trouble about ghosts after death, when life itself is haunted by ghosts so much more terrible?
—CHEKHOV, *Notebooks* (1892–1904)

Contents

Preface

This book has four interrelated themes that follow through and connect what at first glance seem meandering chapters: being haunted by parents; the difficulties of knowing and owning; change meaning loss; the metaphor of the garden.

My title, *Haunted by Parents,* relates to what I have been writing about the continuing importance of early parenting as a source of health and of pathology—a subject of little theoretical controversy for those engaged in psychological therapy. It *is* a given, but I feel that it is not so familiar to the general public. There has not been enough emphasis on holding on to the mental ties to early parents as one powerful motivating force for resistance to change in life as well as in psychiatric treatment. We are all haunted by parents, but with different intensities and each in our own way. I am dealing here with those in whom the results of the haunting are profound. The book should also be of interest to those who are not, and have not been, patients in deep psychotherapy.

Patients, in order to achieve optimal positive psychic changes, need to become consciously and responsibly aware of, and be able to feel fully and learn to *own,* the extent of their inner psychic links to their parents and to their past. I stressed the need for exploration of the power of continuing parental attachment in my last book (Shengold, 2000). For many of my patients who get into situations of near stalemate in long analytic treatments, feeling responsible for these regressive ties requires much interpretation to, and emotional struggle for, the patient. The need to cling to early bonds to parents arouses such strong resistance to change in life as well as in therapy.

The impetus for this book was an invitation from the New York Psychoanalytic Institute to be the Heinz Hartmann Scholar for 2001. (Heinz Hartmann was perhaps the foremost theorist of the American Freudian psychoanalytic school of ego psychology. Many of his contributions were written with Ernst Kris and Rudolph Loewenstein.) Part of my assignment was to deliver an honorary lecture, which has now burgeoned into this book. I thank my colleagues at the New York Psychoanalytic Institute for honoring me with their flattering and evocative invitation.

For much of my information about gardens I am grateful to the editors of the *Oxford Companion to Gardens* (1986). My brilliant internist, Dr. Flavia Golden, is to be thanked for suggesting that Benjamin Spock's life and writings would fit the theme of my book. My discovery of the writings of the great Russian nineteenth-century writer Sergei Aksakov came when reading Esther Salaman's excellent book about memory and autobiography, *The Great Confession* (1973). I profited greatly from Andrew Durkin's fine (1983) book on Aksakov. I am indebted to the psychoanalyst Bonnie Asnes for pointing out to me Edna St. Vincent Millay's poem "Scrub." In dealing with Millay, I owe much to Nancy Milford's well-documented and astute recent (2001) biography of Millay and to Daniel Epstein's (2001) perceptive and passionate book on the poet's life and her love poems, *What Lips My Lips Have Kissed*. I have also found Anne Cheney's (1975) *Millay in Greenwich Village* very useful.

I learned a great deal about Leonard Woolf that supplemented his autobiographical books from reading George Spater's and Ian Parsons's *A Marriage of True Minds* (1977), Natania Rosenfeld's (2000) *Outsiders Together: Virginia and Leonard Woolf, 1941–1968,* Judith Adamson's (2001) *Love Letters: Leonard Woolf and Trekkie Ritchie Parsons,* and from Frederic Spotts (1989), whose commentary on his finely edited collection *Letters of Leonard Woolf* is full of insight and wisdom. They are all excellent books. My speculations are based on their work. I was greatly indebted in writing about Wordsworth to Stephen Gill's (1999) and Kenneth Johnston's (1998) enlightening and marvelous biographies of the poet and Lionel Trilling's (1950) essay "Wordsworth and the Rabbis." I am most grateful to Dr. Alexandra Harrison for permission to quote a transcript of the videotape of a session from her excellent, empathic, and inspiring work with a child patient. I am indebted to the ever-wise psychoanalyst Betty Joseph for several passages I have quoted from her paper on psychic change that anticipate some of my main themes. Last, but not least, I want to thank my wonderful editors at Yale University Press, Keith Condon and Lawrence Kenney.

I

A Literary Example of Haunting: Dr. Benjamin Spock

If I were hanged on the nearest hill,
Mother o' mine, mother o' mine!
I know whose love would follow me still,
Mother o' mine, mother o' mine!

If I were damned of body and soul,
I know whose prayers would make me whole,
Mother o' mine, mother o' mine!
—*Rudyard Kipling, "Mother o' Mine," 1890*

In his "Letter to the Reader of This New Edition" of *Baby and Child Care,* Dr. Benjamin Spock (1957) writes, "When I was writing the first edition [of this book] between 1943 and 1946, the attitude of a majority of people toward infant feeding, toilet training, and general child management was still fairly strict and inflexible. However, the need for greater understanding of children and for flexibility in their care had been made clear by educators, psychoanalysts, and pediatricians, and I was trying to encourage this. Since then a great change in attitude has occurred, and *nowadays there seems to be more chance of a conscientious parent's getting into trouble with permissiveness than with strictness. So I have tried to give a more balanced view*" (Spock 1957, 1–2; emphasis added).[1]

Spock, at forty-three, was writing about having again revised his book, *Baby and Child Care* (first edition, 1946)—eventually issued in millions of copies.[2] (Revisions were written "every eight to ten years" [1985, 35] during the fifty-year interim period up to Spock's death.) There evolved, increasingly, a more balanced view of disciplining children with less emphasis on permissiveness. Throughout, Spock continued to stress basing parental behavior on affection and knowledge of the individual child.

[1] I was led to write this chapter by a conversation with my perceptive, insightful internist, Dr. Flavia Golden, who had asked me what my recently completed book, *Haunted By Parents,* was about. When I briefly described its theme (resistance to change due to the need to hold on to the past and particularly to the mind's conscious and unconscious representation of parents from the past), she talked about the changes of ideas and attitudes of Benjamin Spock. I am very grateful for her relevant suggestion.

[2] The 1957 "revised and enlarged" edition of *Baby and Child Care* states that by that date the book had sold over eight million copies, with decades of successful sales still to come. By 1993, it had sold "over forty million" (Kaye 1993, 9).

Later modifications or even reversals of a thinker's initially unpopular or even revolutionary assertions commonly occur—assertions challenging accepted ideas in science, philosophy, or politics that could influence or have influenced actions and practice.

At ninety-two, Spock wrote a concise autobiographical sketch in his book *A Better World for Our Children* (1995), full of the dependable conscientious honesty and moral courage and fortitude that mark his writings.[3] In his preface, Spock declares his book is about "the deterioration of our society and what caring men and women can do to leave a better world for all our children. The issues I raise in this book have concerned me for many years—as a physician, as a parent and grandparent, as an educator, and as a political activist" (16).

Spock's Childhood

Benjamin Spock was born in 1903, the oldest of six surviving children (the first son, William, had died shortly after birth). Benjamin was "raised in a family where our mother was the dominant influence—for me anyway" (Spock 1995, 19). He recalled few memories from his earliest years, but "by three I had taken on a wistful, mildly anxious look that I ascribe to my sensitivity to the frequent warnings and scoldings of my *moralistic, controlling* mother. She loved her babies extravagantly *but was alarmed when in their second year each of her children showed signs of wishes and wills of their own.* Two of her four daughters became *determinedly independent,* but her two sons were to a rare degree submissive to her will" (1985, 19; emphases added). (Spock himself became actively "determinedly independent"

---

[3] Its subtitle is *Rebuilding American Family Values.*

in many ways in later life when he was consciously trying to fight his tendency to passivity and submission.)[4]

His mother, Mildred, was devoted to her six children and centered her daily life on their care. But in the view of Benjamin's sister Hiddy, "It was perfectly obvious to all of us that [Ben] was the child that she loved [the most]" (quoted in Maier 1998, 10). [5] Kaye (1993) writes of Spock's mother, "She believed in and enforced rigid practices, rules [and] high moral standards. She told Ben and her other children *what to wear, what to eat, and even when to sleep.* For example, unless it was a school day, each child took a nap every day, including holidays" (15; emphasis added).[6] Spock's mother believed that fresh air was essential for a child's good health, and the children all slept on an open sleeping porch in their New Haven home, even on freezing winter nights. Maier (1998) quotes Spock as remarking, "You didn't rebel against fresh air because fresh air was just as sacred as morality" (4).

Mildred appears to have been a severely compulsive, impatient woman who resisted the separation and individuation of her children and insisted on their unwavering obedience. She did not allow any of her children to go to public school until they were seven years old. There was little flexibility in

---

[4] For example, in college he took up rowing and became part of a Yale team that won first place in the 1924 Olympics.

[5] Maier's fine, detailed, and perceptive biography was written in cooperation with Spock and his second wife. He interviewed them both extensively, talked with Spock's children and siblings, and had access to Spock's letters and papers.

[6] She insisted that the children remain vegetarian until they became twelve; and Spock is quoted as saying that, in contrast to the mothers of other children in the neighorhood, "My mother made us stay in. We had to have our baths and be in bed and quiet by 6:45 PM" (Kaye 1993, 17).

her will of iron. Spock (1985) states that his mother "*had [him]* tonsillectomized three times"; the last time he was twenty and in college when "*they* decided that I needed one more. . . . There was no denying my mother" (10; emphasis added). [7] Looking backward in his old age, Spock clearly sees that her children (each, of course, with an unknown different inborn endowment) reacted to their strict upbringing with varying and dynamically changing combinations of rebellion and compliance.

Mildred Spock, characterologically exigent, could also be contradictory. Spock (1985) describes her as filling the house with good books for the children: "Yet if she found me reading, she would immediately find something for me to do— clean up my room, mow the lawn, rake the leaves. So I would find a secret place to read" (44).

Physical closeness, kissing, and hugging within the family were discouraged. And she was hostile to any sexual manifestations: "She taught us that sex was wrong and harmful in all aspects, except when intended to conceive babies.[8] She dearly loved babies.[9] . . . She taught us that sinful thoughts were as

---

[7] Spock (1985): "She *never* doubted that any opinion of hers was other than God's own truth" (63). When he was seventeen, he went to a party against her order and adds, "This was the *first (and last)* time that I dared to defy my mother" (63; emphasis added).

[8] She took on the task of telling her sons "the facts of life" as they became teenagers, stressing the dangers of venereal disease and the terrible physical consequences of masturbation.

[9] Might this statement be ironic? Babies, since she did not see them as sexual, could be loved, but Mildred Spock, as symbiotic ties lessened, was resistant to their progress toward independence. According to Maier, the self-assurance that appears in Spock's early baby pictures disappears from age three on (1998, 7).

harmful as deeds, and to touch ourselves 'down there' was not just sinful but *might cause birth defects in our children*" (Spock 1995, 21; emphasis added). Spock adds that, even after he had been a physician for four or five years, he was surprised to find himself feeling and saying joyfully to his wife that his new-born first child (a son) had ten fingers and ten toes. The new father was able to realize to his surprise that, despite his psycho-analytic and pediatric training, he was still unconsciously haunted by the mother of his childhood.

The reader is not told anything specific in Spock's auto-biographical writings about whether he had been breast- or bottle-fed as an infant or about his toilet training. Nor, except indirectly when he mentions his mother's prohibitions, do we hear anything about his masturbation; these were all topics that were to be dealt with as so important in relation to child development in all editions of Spock's runaway best-selling book *Baby and Child Care.*

The boy had felt his mother was a mind reader who knew what he was thinking, as evidenced by her ability to detect a child's disobedience and wrongdoing immediately: "Only later did I realize that she had implanted such a strong sense of guilt in me that when I occasionally did something slightly naughty, my hang-dog expression was a dead give-away" (21). Spock adds, with the child's frankness and honesty that remained part of his character as an adult, that it never occurred to him to try to deceive her.

Spock gives an example of his mother's "*stern* moral teach-ing" (1995, 22; emphasis added). He was fourteen during World War I, and the government wanted people to conserve wool for the soldiers. His mother insisted on the boy's wearing one of his father's old suits to school. He refused, expecting (and ulti-mately finding) that his schoolmates would laugh at him dressed in adult, ill-fitting clothes.[10] His mother insisted and got her way, saying that the boy should be ashamed to be concerned about what other people thought when he was doing what was right. The powerful, self-righteous woman—tyrant of her household—was given to promoting shame and guilt.

Alongside his registering the resultant chagrin and humiliation, there was a powerful and lasting part of the boy's mind that suppressed his indignation and felt that his mother *was* right. In his narrative, he is obliged to skip forward fifty years and add, in relation to his being arrested[11] for his "vigorous" opposition to the Vietnam War[12]: "I was comforted by recalling my mother's words. I could say to myself, 'It doesn't matter what President Johnson[13] thinks as long as I know I'm right about the illegality, the unconstitutionality of the war in Vietnam.' I knew that my mother would have agreed" (1995, 22).

Yes, one would rejoin, she probably would have. But there is an enormous difference between being forced to acquiesce to what the parent *and not the child* thinks is right and an adult's own defiant refusal to give up, despite threats of punishment, what represents his own conviction. There is the shadow of past parental brainwashing in the passage quoted above—an

---

[10] This narcissistic mortification about clothes burned in his memory. As an adult he was given to buying expensive and dressy clothes for himself and for his first wife, Jane.

[11] He was convicted and sentenced to two years in federal prison. Fortunately, the decision was reversed. Spock was jailed for about a dozen overnight stays during the Vietnam years when he was arrested for "non-violent civil disobedience" (1995, 32).

[12] By then, defiance predominated over compliance and submission to authority.

[13] President Johnson played the role for Spock of the current chief embodiment of the "stern," bad (even, in relation to Vietnam, murderously destructive) but much-needed parent.

unconscious retention of submission to mother's views that existed alongside the adult's firm and courageous resistant stance.

Father

Benjamin remembered his father as having been out of the house a good part of the time and emotionally distant even when he was present. Kaye (1993) quotes Spock as saying that his father "never interfered with mother's discipline" (17). There is no hint that the father ever tried to check his wife's household dominance; perhaps he lacked the strength of character to challenge her. The octogenarian son remembers his father as having been "grave but just" (1985, 14). Father always seemed serious, and we hear of no happy memories in relation to him. The father apparently was sometimes more willing to be friendly, but Benjamin as a child was too afraid of him to respond.[14] Ben's sons once reproached him for not hugging or kissing them when they were children; he told them that he had never been hugged or kissed by his father. (And Ben never saw his parents hugging or kissing.)

There is an absence of joy in Spock's description of his childhood and adolescent family life that suggests "soul murder."[15] As a child, he was almost always the good boy.[16] Spock had felt deep shame at his father's unspoken reproaches (com-

[14] Spock reports that his first wife, Jane, was fatherless, as were two of his earlier girlfriends. He adds, "I must have been unconsciously afraid of jealous fathers" (1965, 71).

[15] See my book *Soul Murder* (1989). Henrik Ibsen in several of his plays (e.g., *John Gabriel Borkman* [1896, 272]) describes "soul murder" as the depriving of another person of joy in life.

[16] Kaye (1993) quotes him as saying, "I never committed an even mildly delinquent act, even on Halloween, and I was considered a goody-goody by the rougher boys in the neighborhood" (20). He was also a mother-adjutant, looking after his younger brother and even changing his diapers.

municated by his facial expression) on the rare occasions of his son's misdemeanors. There was much mutual hostility in the psychic space between father and his oldest son. Maier (1998) writes that Benjamin's sister Hiddy told him, "Neither [brother] got any affection from [father], and they weren't encouraged to give any. He poured affection onto the daughters and denied any to the sons" (18). Spock cites, with characteristic fairness, the contrasting (and his unshared) feelings of father having been "a darling" as recalled by both younger sisters when they were grown up.

Spock (1985) writes when he was eighty-six that his "mother was certainly the person who most influenced my life and my attitudes" (17). But he also felt "Mother was too controlling, too strict, too moralistic. Though I never doubted her love, I was intimidated by her. She controlled her children with a firm and iron hand and complete self-assurance—no hesitation, no permissiveness. She never doubted that she was right in any judgment and never softened a punishment, no matter how piteously the child pleaded. She almost never used physical punishment but relied on deprivation and severe moral disapproval. Her scorn could be *withering*. We all grew up with consciences that were more severe than was necessary or wise" (1985, 18; emphasis added). It is a withering portrait of a parent who seems like a character out of Dickens, a bad mother whose nurture and character cast a shadow over her son's life— like one of Dickens's one-dimensional bad mothers who hated joy (for example, Arthur Clennam's mother in *Little Dorrit*).[17]

Spock and Psychoanalysis

Spock, as a physician interested in child development and as a pediatrician, was strongly influenced by reading Freud—

[17] In the course of the book it is finally revealed to Arthur that she is really his stepmother.

and later by beginning psychoanalytic training, which involved undertaking a psychoanalysis. One can never know specifically what the training analysis (with the master clinician Bertram Lewin) did for him, and how much it helped him come to terms with his relationship to his parents. Spock told his biographer, Maier (1998), that he considered his analysis with Lewin "principally an intellectual exercise rather than an emotional one" (94). He described telling Lewin about his early life with his difficult mother. Lewin must have been dissatisfied with his patient's "guarded self-exploration" (95) since Spock related to Maier that Lewin urged him to try to progress by exploring his dreams. Spock's mother had not appeared in his dreams, although he connected (at least intellectually) his nightmares with her. Spock also describes himself as realizing how afraid he had been of his father. He had previously attributed all of the blame for his unhappiness to his mother. He discovered how much he blamed his father for not protecting him from her and always taking her side against her children.

Spock's disclaimer of deep emotional involvement with the analysis seems contradicted by Maier's statements based on his impression of Spock's description during his interview with him: "[His] rush of forgotten memories struck Ben like a thunderbolt. His personal analysis with Dr. Lewin illuminated dark and unexplored corners of his psyche, parts of his own character Ben had never before considered. His remaining doubts about Freud disappeared" (95). It is a puzzling contradiction. Spock certainly was at least partially convinced that he had an Oedipus complex. The discovery of his hostility to his father was helpful here. I speculate that it was not the knowledge of but the depth of his sexual and hostile feelings toward his parents, especially toward his mother, that was insufficiently felt. Ben's rage as a child must have threatened to become terrifying, a murderous intensity that, accompanied by terror, needed to be repressed and reacted to with "good boy" behavior. In relation to his Oedipus complex, we also hear, and presumably Maier was told, nothing about Spock's heterosexual, homosexual, and primal scene fantasies and connected memories that would have involved both parents.

Spock, in 1937, after he had abandoned his psychoanalytic training, realized that his experience with Lewin had been "too shallow" (Maier 1998, 113) and made another try at analysis with the well-known psychiatrist Sandor Rado. (There were later subsequent attempts; also he was in a group therapy with his second wife in his last years—when he was in his nineties.)

Whatever the deficiencies of his analyses may have been, it seems likely that Spock's initial bias for permissiveness toward babies and children was a reaction to his recalling the details of his Spartan childhood with greater emotional depth as they came to renewed emotional life in the transference toward his analysts. He was haunted by the stern agenda of "She who must be obeyed," to use H. Rider Haggard's phrase (from his novel *She*) (1886, 81).

Although he did not continue with his psychoanalytic career, his analytic training made him familiar with Freudian ideas, and his working with analytic patients in his training must have taught him something about learning how to listen that enhanced his natural psychological-mindedness and empathy. When he was later approached to write a guide for parents about the physical and psychological development of children, he describes himself as trying to integrate what he had learned from Freud with what the mothers he was seeing told him about their babies. He was especially interested in breast and bottle feeding, weaning and toilet training. He writes, "There was no doubt in my mind that Freud and the babies were both

right, but it took me years to find the way to reconcile them"
(1995, 27). His listening and observations enabled him to syn-
thesize the two sources of information and form his own con-
clusions. Later, ten years after writing his first version of *Baby
and Child Care*, Spock was appointed to the departments of
both psychiatry and pediatrics at Western Reserve University
in Cleveland.[18] He set up a joint study by pediatricians and
psychoanalysts of "some still-controversial aspects of child development—the same persistent difficulties with breast feeding, resistance to weaning and toilet training, the meaning of
'security blankets' and stuffed animals that I had written about
in *Baby and Child Care*" (1995, 30).[19]

Saying No to Children

Spock wrote in his Cardinal Giant edition of *Baby and Child
Care* (1957), "If parents are too hesitant in asking for reasonable
behavior—because they have misunderstood theories of self-
expression, because they are self-sacrificing by nature, or because
they are afraid of making their children dislike them—they
can't help resenting the bad behavior that comes instead. They
keep getting angrier underneath, without knowing what to do
about it. This bothers the child, too. It makes him feel guilty
and scared, but it also makes him meaner and all the more demanding" (6). This balanced statement, far from encouraging
permissiveness, shows that harm can ensue if the parent doesn't
or can't say no as well as yes. Spock recognized that the child
can be led by fear of its rage toward a repetitive provocation of

[18] He held the position for the next twelve years.
[19] It may be significant that there is no mention here of infantile masturbation, about which he had so much to say and wrote about with common sense and empathy.

parental anger, alongside or instead of suppressing that rage. The provocation can be mishandled and overreacted to by denial, especially if the parents are also afraid of their own hostility. The child also becomes frightened of losing control of his rage since he can feel that the intensity of his hostility may harm or even kill the parent. The child then will turn rage inward toward himself and becomes full of conscious or unconscious guilt or both that is often manifested by a need for punishment. A vicious mutual sadomasochistic cycle can result.[20]

The Accusation of Overpermissiveness

Several weeks after Spock's indictment for his anti–Vietnam War activities, he was charged by the then well-known cleric Norman Vincent Peale (an ardent backer of the war) with "'corrupting an entire generation.' In a sermon widely reported in the press, Reverend Peale blamed *me* for all the lack of patriotism, lack of responsibility, and lack of discipline of the young people who opposed the war. All these failings, he said, were due to my having told their parents to give them 'instant gratification' as babies" (Spock 1995, 32). Spock adds that the accusation occurred twenty years after his best-selling book was first published, and he believes this attack in 1968 was motivated by the reaction to his politics rather than by his pediatric advice. Still, this public censure by a popular (and self-righteous) parental figure must have evoked Spock's rage and, perhaps, also reactivated the old neurotic guilt and sense of wickedness that stemmed from his mother's accusations and bad expectations of him when he was a child.[21]

---

[20] I will write more about this in subsequent chapters.

[21] George Orwell might have seen Dr. Peale as a lover and justifier of Big Brother.

Strictness or Permissiveness

In his 1995 book, Spock (then ninety-two) wrote about his evolved views on strictness versus permissiveness. Spock, throughout the many rewrites of *Baby and Child Care*, was trying to keep a balanced attitude toward the two contrary directions that parents can (and need to) take in raising their children. Initially, in the forties, when he was writing his widely popular book, his stress was on breaking with and modifying the influence of enforced schedules that had prescribed parental strictures, childhood obedience, and deprivations of gratification (equated with spoiling and overindulgence).

The thinking that had dominated pediatric thought and advice for so many decades took little heed of a child's individual needs, endowment, or identity. At worst, this philosophy of child development fostered a totalitarian household atmosphere that discouraged warm, emotional exchange and empathy. Spock's beliefs and observations led him to emphasize the central importance of empathic permissiveness. The emphasis diminished as he grew more experienced. The need for firmness and flexibility had always been seen. But, in the later editions of his book, the dangers of spoiling and the need for a parental firm but kind no! alongside a firm but kind yes! were increasingly stressed. Here is a relevant statement, made when he was ninety-two, entitled, "Too Many Gifts": "Most American parents (*including me*) give all the gifts their children ask for, whether or not they are sensible, whether or not they can really afford all of them. It expresses their delight in their children, and that is good. But telling the department store Santa Claus every plaything they want and then having a frenzy of opening the presents on Christmas morning encourages a selfish and greedy attitude" (155; emphasis added). Spock adds that a few presents and encouraging children to give and make presents for others can help cultivate kindness and caring in the child. The need to counter his mother's inflexible severity is moderated by his seeing the virtue of limits and rules. He adds something from his personal past that shows an appreciation of the positive side of encouraging gift-giving in building character that was based on his own activity: "I remember well my *joy* in making for my parents, in school, a stack of three small blotters tied with a ribbon [that I decorated with] a small calendar and a picture I had drawn of a house with a winding path leading up to it and a winding wisp of smoke coming out of the chimney." There is poignancy in the image; the child draws a warm and presumably a happy house—with a path, perhaps for the Prodigal Son he wanted but didn't dare to be. He continues: "And I remember *my wild impatience* waiting for my parents to unwrap my gift" (1995, 155–56; emphasis added).[22] One cannot help fearing that the wild impatience and joy would have been crushed by the lack of parental enthusiasm. Spock doesn't tell the reader how they reacted. But he wants him to be aware that "greediness shouldn't *be whipped up* by parents in their asking for lists of all the presents wanted" (156; emphasis added).[23]

---

[22] The psychoanalyst Robert Fliess characterized (wisely, in my view) impatience as "the cannibalistic affect" (1956, 107).

[23] Although Spock's parents were apparently not given to beating or whipping him, I speculate that the use of this metaphor in relation to "greediness" expresses unconscious revival of the child's masochism and need for punishment in relation to his suppressed "impatient" wishes to be loved. Joy was not encouraged. In middle age, Mildred Spock often beat her youngest daughter, Sally, and treated her most sadistically.

The Reappearance of Strict Regimens

Spock and his first wife were divorced after almost fifty years of marriage when their children were grown up. Their marriage had started off as a happy one. (Jane Spock took part in the initial writing of *Baby and Child Care.*) Ben dictated to her and she gave him many suggestions. She initiated the separation—having become mentally ill and alienated by Spock's putting his patients before his family.[24] Spock writes that he can see that his preoccupation with his medical work (and later with his political activism) involved his being away from home so often; this made him a neglectful husband and father despite himself.[25] His frequent moving of the family from city to city with his change of jobs had repeatedly separated the children from their friends. Spock's self-accusation in relation to his fatherhood, whatever its validity, would seem to me to show his identification with his own physically and emotionally absent father.

It is a shock to read about his difficulties with his own children and his comparative neglect of them; about his disapproval of sexuality expressed by the need to interfere with his son John's wrestling with a friend that seems to have had homosexual connotations for him; and about his obeying his second wife's compulsive regimen in the frugality and abstinence of his old age.

[24] Maier writes (1995) that Jane Spock was "a strong, opinionated woman" (117), as was his second wife, Mary. Jane could be considerate and obedient, but she also knew how to get her way.

[25] I have discovered, on presenting a short version of this chapter in more than one city, that Spock had the reputation, toward the end of his first marriage, of being a womanizer. More than one middle-aged woman in the audiences claimed to have been fondled and propositioned by him.

In his old age, and apparently partially guided by the beliefs and decisions of his beloved second wife, Mary Morgan, "an Arkansan with an energetic and determined personality" (Spock 1995, 35), Spock and Mary embarked on a program of diet, meditation, exercise, group discussion of problems, and, especially important, a macrobiotic diet.[26] This was excellent for their health, and it perhaps prolonged Spock's life. It did involve a strict (although probably not a "stern" regimen) that sounds as if it might have been a benevolent repetition of his childhood life with mother. The couple's day was planned out in obsessive detail. Their daily routine started with waking "without an alarm clock" (1995, 38) at some time between five and six A.M. There followed three hours of transcendental meditation, yoga, arm and leg exercises, and massage. After this, "we have a macrobiotic breakfast. We *always* begin with a miso soup followed by a whole-grain dish—brown rice, whole oats, buckwheat, millet, quinoa, wheat berries, barley.... I eat leafy greens 3 times a day ... *always* removed from the heat after 2 or 3 minutes so they stay bright green. Our exercise *each day* is a 30 minute swim.... We also walk for 10 to 15 minutes after our meals. By 9:00 P.M. we are ready to go to bed. ... We also do a weekly group therapy session" (1985, 38–40; emphasis added). Compare this with Spock's (1995) statement about his childhood: "We children *always* had an early supper at a childrens' table, which was much lower than my knees by the time I was eleven and still sitting at it. Supper would typically be cereal and applesauce. It was served *always* at 5:30 P.M. Our mother made us stay in. We had to have our baths and be quiet by 6:45 P.M." (7; emphasis added).

---

[26] Spock felt that Mary looked like his mother and wore her hair in the same style; Mary took this as a compliment (see Maier 1998, 438).

Spock was haunted by his parents, mainly by his mother. But his living intrapsychically with his mother and *as* his mother, even after her death, was increasingly moderated—benevolently transformed—as he matured; gradually passivity gave way to activity. These trends were augmented by Spock's skill as a physician, by his psychoanalysis, by his well-appreciated creative writing, by his becoming a husband and a father. But the haunting remained. It is a paradox. The achievement and heroic success of the author of *Baby and Child Care* were in part the result of his having identified with the independence and willfulness of his spirited mother. He became a champion of the rights of children, a rebel at the time of the war in Vietnam (even running for president himself on an independent party ticket). He was (again, like his mother) a lover of babies, and he became a dedicated, empathic physician to his patients.[27] Haunting can turn out to result in good as well as bad. Spock (1985) wrote the following panegyric: "I get my optimism, perhaps my most useful quality, from all the love and good food I received in my first year. From my mother's fierce independence of thought, her scorn for following the crowd, I surely got my independence in making up my own mind that enabled me to pioneer in the psychological aspects of pediatric practice, to see the desperate need for disarmament, to condemn Lyndon Johnson's escalation of the war in Vietnam. It was her idealism that inspired the same perspective in all her children" (21).

But his sense of identity and independence were also so compromised by his mother's disciplinary parenthood (unmodified by his indifferent father). He was not always able to

---

[27] Spock (1995) wrote about his taking on so much diapering of and feeding his newborn brother, Bob, when Ben was nine: "That summer's experience identifying with Mother in her love of babies was no doubt the main influence in my decision, a dozen years later, to go into pediatrics" (4).

control the need for reactive submission to his mother or care as much as he wanted to about his first wife, his children, and perhaps most of all about himself. It is sad that, celebrated and famous at age eighty-six, he needed to write about the impact of his mother's strictness and tyranny on his mind and emotions: "All my life, up to this day, I've felt guilty until proven innocent" (1985, 18).

II

A Clinical Illustration of Some of My Main Themes

He despises what he sought; and he seeks
that which he lately threw away.
—*Horace,* Epistles *I:I:90*

Patient X came to see me for his second attempt at psycho-analysis because several years after completing the first with another analyst he still felt "saddled with" fantasies of beating and being beaten. Sadomasochistic practices had been considerably reduced during his first analysis. But anal arousal, beating fantasies, and masturbation associated with them persisted. He realized he both wanted and did not want to give them up. The ambivalence (involving "evil" impulses) troubled this formerly deeply religious man. He seemed to have learned what his conflicts were, but his knowing, in my view, was largely intellectual and not responsible for (not an *owning* of) them. He no longer went to church but with and following his analysis seemed to have substituted obsessing and thinking about his desires for the relief that going to confession used to give him. During the first year of his reanalysis, X repeatedly asserted, "Change is loss!" He had been in a church choir as a boy and subsequently had studied and remained fond of music. X was sometimes obsessively preoccupied with melodies or parts of them, and these often appeared in his associations. One musical theme he sang out more than once during his analytic hours was the words accompanying four staccato notes that begin a recitative from part 1 of Handel's *Messiah:* "And sudden-ly. . . ."[1] His singing would usually be followed by a short pause. When first asked about this leitmotif, X became anxious and kept silent. Eventually he connected the musical pronouncement with sudden changes in the facial expressions and behavior of his "intermittently crazy" mother that preceded or occurred during her slapping or beating of him; good mother had *suddenly* become bad. Later on, X, no longer so obsessed with musical phrases, began mentally "collecting" what he called his "And suddenly phenomena," past and current. The most compelling of these was the precipitant change from erotic pleasure to painful and frightening overstimulation, during the frequent enemas his mother had, when he was a child, forced on him. "She was addicted to enemas," X explained.

X had been molested as a boy, masturbated and perhaps anally fondled by an adult choirmaster. He remembered no penetration and said he had had no subsequent homosexual

---

[1] "And suddenly there was with the angel a multitude of the heavenly host praising God" (1742, iv). Unlike X's "suddenly," this marks a moment of joy. The angel has just announced the birth of Jesus.

contacts. Bitterness about the sexual abuse had been part of his rationalization for leaving the Catholic Church.

X was not married. He had had a few short, casual heterosexual affairs, but his adult sexual life consisted mostly of one-night stands with women he picked up in bars. There had never been much more than a sadistic kind of role-playing in his sexual acts. He had always avoided enacting what appeared to be the more frightening and destructive details of his sadomasochistic fantasies. These details were not consciously experienced with anxiety; this was consistent with his predominant mode of not knowing (by emotional nonacceptance of) what he could acknowledge as being present or as having been experienced.

X also had platonic friendships with women toward whom he had "almost fraternal" feelings of closeness. But there were only a few people about whom he felt warmly, and he often would avoid contact with the small number of friends with whom he kept in touch. X experienced moments of mild paranoid reaction in relation to authority figures, and these began to appear toward me in the analysis. He would occasionally try to provoke me to reject and punish him.

When driving his car, he was likely to exceed speed limits and had repeatedly jeopardized his license by getting too many speeding tickets. But X was quite talented and generally successful in his work—yet he had somehow avoided the kind of advancement and achievement that his accomplishments ought to have assured.

As X was about to start his session on a day in May toward the end of the first year of his analysis with me, I told him what days I was going to miss on the forthcoming Memorial Day and Fourth of July holidays. I also announced the dates of my August vacation. X was used to my making occasional statements of approaching changes in my schedule at the start of a session, and he had been accustomed to his first analyst's taking August off. But I was aware that my declaration (involving the prospect of the first long separation from me) could easily have evoked an "And suddenly phenomenon." Indeed, X told me the next day that he had heard the four notes during the session but had not reported it.

A Garden Dream

X went on to tell me that the night between the two analytic hours he had had a strange dream that he could only vaguely remember. Some figure representing Death had appeared in a garden. X had no visual memory of the figure, and the specifics of the garden setting were not clear. There had been a general sense of greenness. Groups of people were walking about in the garden. Some of them may have been dead. He was alone among these weird strangers and yet had felt little fear. "I was there as a kind of indifferent witness. There were some people there that I seemed to know, but I wasn't sure. You were NOT in it," he said. I felt that this emphasis marked what Freud calls a negation: it meant I *was* in it.

X then told me that the anniversary of his mother's death was approaching. Sadly, she who had always said she wished to die as an old lady in her garden had actually been killed in her early fifties in an urban highway accident—another dreadful "and suddenly!"

X next talked about several meetings he had recently attended that were in one way or another designed to honor well-known people, some living and some dead. One was a lecture by a professional rival whom he regarded as an enemy. Hatred of or from an enemy didn't bother him much, but it was different if he felt antagonism toward a friend. X then recounted a recent discussion with an old (and an older) friend, B, in which X had made an embarrassing slip of the tongue. "I meant to tell B that I had been happy to hear about the forthcoming appearance of a celebratory volume to be published on the occasion of his birthday, but what came out was 'for your memorial volume.' 'But I'm not dead,' B responded with a laugh. 'Oh, my God!' I cried, and I apparently looked so stricken, that B hugged me, and we were almost in tears. It was a poignant moment."

I pointed out to X that my announcement about holidays and vacation had been followed by his dream about separation and death, and that his associations to the dream had led up to an obvious death wish toward someone he cared about. X followed my logic and agreed, but he was not ready at that time to accept responsibly (and own), at least in relation to me, what his intellect told him was true.

When X was seven, both his parents, after returning from a vacation in South America, became seriously ill with a rare tropical infection and had to be hospitalized for a long period. The boy was suddenly[2] sent away from his home city to be cared for by an aunt and uncle who he felt hated him and whom he hated. They had no children, and X felt certain that neither wanted him in their home. He was frequently severely beaten by his capricious and choleric uncle, supposedly for disobedience.[3] More than once X had been left with bruises. He had known his parents were sick, yet that wasn't enough to excuse

---

[2] This was one of the early, and most memorably bitter, items in his "collection."

[3] X thought it was more likely to have been that he was beaten according to the malevolent whim of his "paranoid" uncle—occasions for many "And Suddenly Phenomena."

them. X had the guilt-ridden thought that they should never have permitted all this to happen; this had hurt more than the physical pain of the beatings. X's happiest times in his exile were when he was allowed to play by himself in a large walled garden. The garden resembled his mother's garden at home; both were apparently modeled on the maternal grandparents' garden. He remembered his grandparents as having been so kind. Why hadn't he been sent to live with them? Perhaps his grandmother had already died by then. But perhaps she had been ill when they started out on that vacation. He wasn't sure. X subsequently reported that in his dreams and thoughts he still kept going back to his "crazy, mean, paranoid" uncle's house. He added, "You would say that I really want to be back there again, but that is not so." (Another negation.)

The undifferentiated green garden background in the dream led X to speak of a scene from Laurence Olivier's movie of Shakespeare's *Henry the Fifth*, which he had seen when he was young. It was the scene of the death of Falstaff, in which Mistress Quickly describes the fat old man dying in his bed, occupied with flowers and prattling of green fields: "Hostess. Nay, sure, he's not in hell. He's in Arthur's bosom, if ever man went to Arthur's bosom. A' made a finer end and went away an it had been any christome child.[4] A' parted ev'n just between twelve and one, ev'n at the turning of the tide. For after I saw him fumble with the sheets, and play with flowers, and smile upon his finger's end, I knew there was but one way. For his nose was as sharp as a pen, and a' babbled of green fields" (*Henry V*, II, iii, 8–16). The actress who spoke the lines had been very moving, and the scene had made X weep. (I felt this Falstaffian association was a clear allusion not only to X's overweight

---

[4] Christome = just christened.

uncle, but also to his somewhat portly analyst. I said nothing, hoping X would come to these connections on his own.)[5]

I had other thoughts here that I did not share with my patient. I found myself remembering a dying Polish lady from the cancer ward in which I once worked as an intern. She used to say to me in her thick accent, with intense yearning, "Please dear, take me out to the green meadows! I want to see the garden and the flowers." I felt she might have been remembering the meadows of her youth, wanting perhaps to die in the garden of her childhood in Poland; maybe, I had speculated, she unconsciously wanted to go back to and join her dead mother there. These old thoughts seem to have been evoked by my awareness of X's mother's desire to die in her garden and of X's own ambivalence toward his mother, wanting both to join her in death and to be rid of her and her "craziness."[6] And now, with the approaching separation, he wanted to get rid of me for abandoning him and yet was afraid of losing me. A young child fears that its intense anger has the power to kill—due to the terrifying magic force of his early emotion-laden wishes (the fulfillment of which would bring unbearable loss). This conflict-ridden concentration was being revived in the relation to the analyst (transference)—as it had previously been revived in the sudden separation at seven. In the dream, the terrifying intensities had been defensively reduced to the indifference of a casual onlooker.

[5] X initially had some of the coldheartedness of Henry the Fifth, who as Prince Hal had acted the role of bosom companion of the wicked but lovable Falstaff. But after Henry's coronation he spurned the fat, old knight: "I know thee not, old man: fall to thy prayers;/How ill white hairs become a fool and jester!" (*Henry the Fourth, Part II*, V, v, 52–54).

[6] Later in this book I will have more to say about the significance of gardens.

Resistance to Change, In and Out of Psychoanalysis

X was as resistant to change in the emotional attachments revived by his psychoanalytic treatment as he had been in his previous life. The feeling that change means loss is, of course, not limited to patients in psychiatric treatment. Such assumptions are there to varying degrees in all of us. Many people live lives that appear to be full of variety, yet in their emotional relation to others it is a matter of *plus ça change, plus c'est la même chose* (the more things change, the more they remain the same).[7] For example, Mozart's (and Da Ponte's) Don Giovanni seduces one woman after another—but his continual change in sexual partners of every variety invariably ends up with each of them reduced to a name in the book his servant Leporello carries containing a long list of his master's sexual conquests.

[7] Another example of the French proverb, with complicated dynamic variations, is described in chapter 9 dealing with the life of the poet Edna St. Vincent Millay.

III

Knowing, Change, and Good and Bad Expectations

LADY BRACKNELL. *I have always been of the opinion that a
man who desires to get married should know either everything
or nothing. Which do you know?*
JACK. *(after some hesitation). I know nothing, Lady Bracknell.*
LADY BRACKNELL. *I am pleased to hear it. I do not approve of
anything that tampers with natural ignorance.*
—Oscar Wilde, The Importance of Being Earnest

My book requires a kind of *apologia,* defined by
Webster's as "a written defense of a writer's principles or conduct; a work written as a justification for one's motives, convictions or acts"
(1989, 70). One of its epigraphs and a chapter title is a well-

known quotation, "Que sçais-je?" (What do I know?) from Michel de Montaigne (1580), the great sixteenth-century French writer whose *Essays* have been bedside reading for a good part of my life. He is, to use psychoanalytic jargon, an ego ideal.[1] My meandering style, fondness for quotations, and tendency toward personal references are in large part derived from Montaigne. I have tried (not always successfully, as the reader will see), consistent with maintaining an endeavor to be natural and open, to limit personal references in my writings as being generally inappropriate for psychoanalysts, whose *relative* anonymity is important for patients who might hear or read their work.

As I, as lecturer and writer, get further and further beyond the status of what W. B. Yeats (1928) calls "a sixty-year-old smiling public man" (240), I seem to be living out a paradox. After all my years of work I am beginning to feel that I generally know what I am doing. Yet I am increasingly aware of, and hopefully coming to terms with, how much I do not know. In presenting my recent writings in public (including early versions of some of my chapters in this book), I have heard contradictory responses from the audience about the quality of my ideas. I have been enthusiastically thanked, with someone remarking that what I had to say made something clear that, once pointed out, was obviously true. This observation has, more than once, been followed by a curmudgeon's (from the same audience) expressing something similar transformed by a tone of scornful, accusatory complaint: for example, "We already *know* what you are telling us!" I think both responses

---

[1] An ego ideal is someone on whom one wishes to and tries to model oneself.

have merit. I am again going to dwell on a few observations that are not original and more philosophic or generally psychological than psychoanalytic.

Fear of Change

Over the past decade I have been doing mostly second and third (re-)analyses. During this time, I have become convinced that feeling and transmitting the emotional force of some familiar generalizations about the mind is frequently central to the understanding of the conflicting *motivations* of many patients who get mired down in long, seemingly interminable psychotherapeutic treatments. These patients neither require nor want supportive therapy yet appear to be persistently resistant to deepening and becoming responsible for what they already know and to exploring the unknown. They generally resist change, including and often featuring change for the better. Stubborn resistance persists, despite these patients' obvious capacity or even talent for psychoanalytic work.

In a paper written in 1986, Betty Joseph wrote,

> Patients come into analysis because they are dissatis-
> fied with the way things are; and they want to alter, or
> want things to alter. There is a desire for change and
> pressure toward greater integration; without it analy-
> sis would fail. And yet there is a dread of change. Un-
> consciously they know that the change that they ask
> for involves an internal shifting of forces, a distur-
> bance of an established mental and emotional equi-
> librium, a balance unconsciously established of feel-
> ings, impulses, defenses and internal figures, which is
> mirrored in their behavior in the external world. . . .

Our patients unconsciously sense this and tend therefore to feel the whole process of analysis as potentially threatening.[2] This is, of course, essentially linked with Freud's ideas on resistance. (193)

Such patients seem compelled to cling to their neurosis, and especially to their neurotic early emotional attachments (Joseph's "internal figures"). They usually need a very long time or more than one analysis in order to diminish their resistances. They are motivated to keep the analysis (and especially the relationship with the analyst) going, but not to work in it toward liberating change, tending to avoid or defer the modifications they initially declared they wanted to make. To fight through the stalemate of resistance, they need to achieve and learn to bear the emotional conviction that would transform mere intellectual and theoretical acceptance of what they claim they already know into insight that has motivational force. Only emotional conviction can supply that force. And for that one must be able to feel and tolerate concomitant forbidden and psychologically dangerous emotions that, repudiated in consciousness, lurk in the mind to be felt. Knowing, with being able to accept that such emotional resonances exist, allows for what I have called *owning* insight.[3] Sometimes the feelings can be recognized in others yet not acknowledged (in responsible consciousness) as applicable to oneself. One patient remarked, "I know that you are only repeating what I have already told you about my parents, and I know that it is true, but I just

[2] Betty Joseph, I feel sure, would agree with me that although the dread of change is universal, every individual has his or her own dynamic quantum and unique configuration of it.

[3] I first heard the word "owning," used in the sense I have defined it, from Anna Freud.

won't accept it." The freedom to own what is there to be felt, especially about self and parents (and about the analyst in transference), can take a long period of working through.[4]

Emotional Varieties of Knowing

The great French religious philosopher Simone Weil wrote, "Belief in the existence of other human beings as such is love" (quoted in Auden and Kronenberger 1962, 90). We can know that others exist, but there is a range of meaningfulness in such knowledge; knowing does not always feature love as defined by Weil. It can involve an intense hatred that denies part of the other's humanity, or defensive indifference—the other reduced to a statistic or a category.[5] I will illustrate a range of depths of knowing that shows an increasing ability to empathize—to know with feeling:

1. The reaction to reading a newspaper item about thousands of deaths caused by a hurricane in a distant foreign place;
2. The reaction to seeing the corpses of some of the victims on television;
3. The reaction of an American seeing a man hanging out of a high-story window of a World Trade

[4] "Working through" refers to the patient's need to repeat emotional conflicts over and over in life. When repeated and repeatedly interpreted in relation to the analyst in the course of the analysis, this can, eventually, result in a gradual attainment of emotional conviction that allows for owning. This requires much patience from both patient and analyst.

[5] A few years ago I saw a television interview of the ex-mistress of a concentration camp commandant. He would sometimes, as a kind of sport, shoot and kill one of the prisoners from his balcony. When asked how she could stand being a witness, she answered in a tone of sincere righteousness, "You don't understand. They were *Jews!*"

Center tower in an attempt to escape the flames on September 11, 2001;

4. The reaction of a New Yorker who had a friend, lover, or relative (sibling, parent, child) in that tower;
5. Being in the tower oneself after the plane's explosive contact.[6]

In relation to the range of crescendo in my examples, it is most likely that defenses against owning will be brought into play against the least affecting and the most affecting—the first because there is too little emotional impact, and the last because there is too much.

Defenses

To describe not owning or not accepting what may still stay in intellectual conscious awareness requires using many of the arbitrarily defined metaphors psychoanalysts call mechanisms of defense, like repression, suppression, isolation, denial, disavowal, dissociation, splitting. I call them metaphors because the ways people defend themselves psychologically that are encountered in any individual patient are so varied and complex. I am convinced that no amount of trying to find exact "scientific" definition of these terms can obviate the fact that we *all*, patients and analysts alike, have our own idiosyncratic dynamic medley of many ways of not responsibly knowing.[7]

---

[6] This last and most intense narcissistic level of owning was an addition suggested by Dr. Lee Grossman.

[7] There is a compulsion to repeat these defenses. I have observed that some patients talk about a traumatic "memory" and then follow with "Maybe I just made that up." This doesn't validate that there has been trauma, but it does show a need, which requires explanation, for the repetition of compulsive doubting.

Betty Joseph (1986) writes, "I am stressing not just the obvious point that all our patients use different defense mechanisms, but that the interlocking of their defenses is so fine that shifts in one area must always cause disturbances in another, and that a major part of achieving change lies in our trying to unravel within the analysis the various layers and interlockings so that they may be re-experienced and opened up within the transference" [upon the analyst] (193). The patient must get to know *that* and, specifically *how,* he or she is refusing to know and own what is purported to be already known. Not accepting what one registers in a walled-off compartment in the mind is often, but not always, a subtle defense. (I will say more about owning in a separate chapter.)

I am aware of the danger of complacency about being or appearing humble that can negate arrogance or cover over simplemindedness (Lady Bracknell's sometimes admirable "natural ignorance"). Yet I am going to stick my neck out by stressing one of these homilies—change means loss—as being connected with specific clinical and literary material centering on some dark connotations of hope and promise, promise as exemplified in spring and the approach of summer with its flowers and gardens.

The Genetic Principle: Crucial Beginnings and Expectations

Most psychoanalysts believe in what has been called the genetic principle: what occurs early in physiological and in psychic development is and continues to be of momentous importance—the earlier the occurrence, the greater the effect (see appendix 2).[8]

---

[8] Karl Abraham once illustrated the genetic principle by pointing out the grievous consequences of sticking a pin into an early embryo as compared to the insignificant ones if the same is done to a child.

Every beginning patient in analysis faces expectations of an unknown and unprecedented procedure and relationship. Every new patient provides the analyst with a new adventure, a new "unexplored region of the mind" (Freud 1954, 318) to investigate—a region of which the analyst and the patient together will try to "draw . . . [a] crude map" (Freud 1954, 245). The excitement of this prospect of the new is one of the privileges of being a psychological therapist. Every individual and every individual mind is unique, and recognizing this is part of the caring and loving attention the therapist should try to bring to the patient. Hopefully the patient will eventually share some of this positive feeling about what is new. But novelty and surprise prove so often to be predominantly a threat, especially for the beginning patient. We all tend to be wary of change as a risk that can imperil our stability, jeopardizing our link to adjustments and dependencies preserved from the past.

We are all burdened with our own idiosyncratic load of bad expectations that have evolved and then, in the course of development, become transformed for better or worse. But the early threats of danger and loss never disappear, and even infantile terrors can be maintained or regressively revived in the adult. The early dangers are clamorous, threatening overstimulation (too-muchness—having to bear the unbearable), menacing one's earliest identifications and psychic ties to parents and consequently to one's sense of identity. Most adults can, most of the time, keep the anxieties attached to regarding change as loss at an attenuated level, useful as signals of danger. Such signals can even function unconsciously and fairly automatically. But the new and especially the unexpected tend to evoke excessive anxiety in some people.

The analyst or therapist is in the active position of the parent who sets the rules. He or she has an inexact but fairly good general grasp of the varieties of ways in which the analytic situation will be likely to develop. Frequently for the beginning psychological therapist and almost invariably for the patient—even for the former analytic patient who is starting with a new analyst—there is a feeling of considerable vulnerability. Every patient is in the position of the child who will, if the therapy is going to be meaningful, begin to feel emotionally dependent on the analytic therapist. The neurotic underpinnings of the dependency will be strengthened by the regression fostered by the development, in an analytic treatment that works, of a rather full revival of the feelings and expectations from childhood (joy, sorrow, loves, hatred, anger, danger, helplessness, dread) that first centered on the patient's parents. For the patient, particularly for the patient who *starts out* the treatment with a heavy load of dreadful anticipations, a new deep emotional involvement can evoke intense anxiety and the various defensive psychic evasions like avoidance, denial, and other various ways of distancing painful feelings. It is paradoxical that even, and for some especially, what promises to be change for the better is soon felt and reacted to as a danger. When change predominantly promises to be loss, change has to be resisted.

The properly trained analyst has been analyzed. This, together with subsequent experience, has not produced miraculous release from neurosis and protection from the vicissitudes of the human condition but should at least have resulted in a relatively good knowledge of his or her neurotic weaknesses. That can be enough to make for proper self-monitoring control and performance with the relatively safe emotional distance required for professional functioning as an analyst. (Functioning as a therapist can be difficult and challenging but is, fortunately, much less emotionally demanding than what goes on in personal life.) At the very least, the knowledge of what it was and is like to be an analytic patient and a beginning analytic patient should have been acquired; one has been there oneself. Luckily, most who chose and are accepted for training as psychoanalytic healers have enough inherent therapeutic talent to allow them to get through their own shaky beginnings of functioning in the active and responsible role of the therapist. Still, the first experiences as psychotherapists are occasions for anxiety, and for some beginners confrontation with a new patient can be quite frightening. Anxiety can exist alongside relative confidence and the pleasurable prospect of a new experience. But some of those anxieties will recur in the therapist's first ventures in doing psychoanalysis, especially when one is still being analyzed. Most who lack the sense of professional identity (the hopefully flexible, professional armor) that can come only with repetitive experiences are, and should be, anxious. (No surgical neophyte would be permitted to operate on a patient with the comparative inexperience of the beginner in psychological therapy or psychoanalysis.) Since such treatment contains no actual physical danger to the patient, common sense, psychological-mindedness, and modest caution get most neophyte therapists through. Fortunately, almost all psychoanalytic trainees begin with sufficient clinical experience to supplement their inborn or early acquired empathic talent and tact; and so, with the help of supervision by experienced analysts, good therapeutic and analytic work can be accomplished even by beginners.

IV
Beginnings and Wordsworth's "Immortality Ode"

Heaven lies about us in our infancy! . . .
At length, the man perceives it die away,
And fade into the light of common day.
— William Wordsworth, "Immortality Ode," 1807

Youth, what man's age is like to be, doth show;
We may our ends by our beginnings know.
— Sir John Denham Of Prudence, (1655)

Freud taught us, according to the (often didactic) poet W. H. Auden, "To remember / Like the old and be honest like children" (1940, 1048). But psychoanalysts inevitably have to cope with that which cannot be remembered—with the dark, psychic developmental mysteries of the early years of life—especially of the first year. We catch fleeting glimpses of those mysteries of the unrememberable when attempting empathic observation of infants and when, in psychoanalytic treatment, we study subsequent patterns of actions and words—patterns motivated partly by what is present in the mind from birth and earliest development.

Wordsworth on the Mind of the Child

William Wordsworth, in his great poem "Intimations of Immortality from Recollections of Early Childhood" (which I think should be assigned reading for anyone interested in child development), beautifully evokes the fervent intensities of the early years of life. The epigraph of the poem is the familiar proto-Freudian quotation, "The Child is father of the Man" (1807, 587).[1] The poet is describing the idealized ("celestial") great sensory and emotional ardor of our earliest years, the great expectations of the springtime of life,[2] when he says of our birth:

. . . trailing clouds of glory do we come
From God who is our home.

(Most psychological scientists would, irrespective of religious belief, substitute [or at least add] "mother and her womb" for "God" here.)

I will quote a somewhat juxtaposed and very shortened version of the poem:

[1] Steven Marcus (1992) writes of "Wordsworth's perceived sense of unconscious thoughts and processes" (1) and reminds us that he used, indeed coined, the word *underconsciousness*. Wordsworth can be seen as a proto-Freudian.

2. Wordsworth mentions May and its promise three times in this poem of 210 lines. For the relevance of this, see chapter 3.

There was a time when meadow, grove, and stream
The earth and every common sight
To me did seem
Appareled in celestial light,
The glory and the freshness of a dream.
It is not now as it hath been of yore;
Turn wheresoe'er I may.
By night or day
The things which I have seen I now can see no more.
. . .
[Change means loss: this is my chorus, not Wordsworth's.]
And all the earth is gay;
Land and sea
Give themselves up to jollity,
And with the heart of May
Doth every beast keep holiday.
. . .
The rainbow comes and goes
And lovely is the Rose . . .
The sunshine is a glorious birth;
But yet I know, where'er I go,
That there hath passed away a glory from the
earth . . .
[Change means loss.]
While Earth herself is adorning
This sweet May morning
And the Children are culling
On every side,
In a thousand valleys far and wide
Fresh flowers . . .

[The poet goes on to remind us how "the prison gates begin to
close" increasingly upon the child as *he* (feminism too was then

in its early childhood) progresses through *boyhood,* youth, *manhood* and old age; Wordsworth then enjoins us as grownups:]

> Ye that through your hearts today
> Feel the gladness of May! . . .

[The adult, the poet says, can still see and appreciate the natural beauty of the world but tells us to remember that:]

> Nothing can bring back the hour
> Of splendour in the grass, of glory in the flower;

[and he asks:]

> Whither is fled the visionary gleam?
> Where is it now the glory and the dream? (1807,
>   587–90).

[Change means loss.]

Wordsworth's moving statement of the experiential loss of the wonderful refulgence of our early years is echoed in analytic theory. Analytic observers of children, supported by their findings (admittedly influenced by psychoanalytic theory), assume that the infant experiences a primal heavenly glory of narcissistic bliss at the breast. The intense good feelings are soon accompanied by correspondingly perfervid sensory and sensual bad feelings (traumatic overstimulation, frustration, pain) that can quickly change the glory to misery. But of course such feelings must be tolerated for us to survive and registered in the mind for us to know and to accept the limitations imposed by human nature and external reality. Freud postulated that our first mental act—one that follows the inevitable frustration of bodily need—is the hallucinatory visual image of that which fulfills the bodily need of satisfaction at the breast. Early experiences of overstimulation of the body (too-muchness—

pain, the dissatisfaction of unfulfilled somatic and erogenous needs, and of the tribulations of somatic dysfunction) also partake of the near hallucinatory sensory intensities of those earliest times. These contradictory powerful perceptions of beginning registration and structuring may be the psychological origin of the concepts of heaven and hell. The dawning of the sense of self, Freud postulates, starts with the mind arising from the body, from what he calls "body ego."[3] These early bodily feelings, sensations and affects, influence our very registration of experience—our mental representations of our bodies and of others and of the external world. This burgeoning of psychic contents from the world mainly within the body at first and then, gradually, the world outside the body is part of the establishment of mental structure—bodily I-ness (body ego) becoming psychic I-ness (psychic ego).

We continue throughout our lives to resonate with those glorious and terrible intensities (intimations of both immortality and mortality) that adhere to the somatically based perceptions and proto-emotions of our earliest existence. These primitive mental contents (as well as corresponding primitive mental functioning) remain in the mind alongside and beneath subsequently achieved modulations and transformations at every developmental phase of progress. They can be revived in situations leading to the need to push threats out of consciousness, especially with the actuality or the anticipation of danger, trauma, and helplessness. As we retreat from our period of the promise of narcissistic glory when, so to speak, we *were* the universe (merged with, or a part of, the God-parent),

---

[3] Body ego means the sense of "I-ness" arising primarily from awareness of one's body.

change increasingly threatens loss of the established but deteriorating position of being the center of creation. Empathic parenting together with good genetic endowment (and predominant good fortune) will, of course, help most of us to be able to balance this bad expectation with the feeling that change, also and even frequently principally, means gain.[4] We all have continuing and dynamically varying mental conflict sparked by these existential expectations.

It is important, in these embattled days for Freudian psychoanalysis, to reaffirm that in the beginning is the body and that the body-ego leads to and continues to influence the subsequent development of psychic ego and eventually the adult mind. We can find affirming comfort in a quote from another great English-speaking poet, Walt Whitman: "Behold! The Body includes and is the meaning . . . and includes and is the soul" (1855b, 105).

Wordsworth, born in 1770, was the second of his parents' five children. His older brother, Richard, had arrived two years previously. His beloved sister Dorothy was born one and a half years later.

In two of his greatest poems, the shorter "Immortality Ode" and the long, autobiographical "The Prelude," Wordsworth presented general (the "Ode") and more specifically personal ("The Prelude") thoughts about the development of mind and creativity in infancy, childhood, and subsequent life. ("The Prelude" was worked on and over for most of the poet's adult life and published in two versions: one in 1805 and the other posthumously in 1850.)

Although both poems present infancy and early child-

---

[4] To use a common simile, some people see a half-filled glass as being half full, others as half empty; some do both.

hood predominantly as a time of great joy, Wordsworth, after his first few years, apparently did not have a preponderantly happy childhood over the next five or six years. The 1799 manuscript version of "The Prelude" describes joy at age four. The poet addresses the river Derwent, picturing himself as a boy standing near or in it. The river flowed past the family garden at Cockermouth, from which the sounds of its falls could be heard:

> . . . a four years' child,
> A naked boy, among thy silent pools
> Made one long bathing of a summer's day,
> Basked in the sun, or plunged into thy streams,
> Alternate, all a summer's day, or coursed
> Over the sandy fields, and dashed the flowers
> Of yellow grunsel; or, when crag and hill,
> The woods, and distant Skiddaw's lofty height
> Were bronzed with a deep radiance, stood alone
> A naked savage in the thunder shower (quoted by
>   Gill 1989, 15)

Gill, one of Wordsworth's biographers, comments that in the 1799 version the poet moves directly from this passage to his contented (sometimes remembered or at least described as ecstatic) school days at Hawkshead, "thus eliding some five years of his childhood" (1989, 15). These five years, from ages three to eight, were apparently sometimes quite unhappy.

The rather grand family home was at Cockermouth in the Lake country, but, from the time William was three or four, the children were often sent away from home to spend long stays at their maternal grandparents' home in nearby Penrith, about eighteen miles away, "periods of time that from a child's perspective must have seemed endless" (Gill 1989, 15). Gill (1989) quotes from some autobiographical notes that the sixty-seven-year-old poet dictated to his nephew in 1847 that revealed suicidal intent at a time when he was with his grandparents in Penrith: "I was of a stiff, moody and violent temper; so much so that I remember going once into the attics of my grandfather's house at Penrith, upon some indignity having been put upon me, with an intention of destroying myself with one of the foils which I knew was kept there. I took the foil in hand, but my heart failed" (15).

Losses

At age eight, there was catastrophe. His mother suddenly died of pneumonia—the first and worst of a series of terrible losses. His beloved sister Dorothy (aged five), already a favorite companion, was promptly sent away from the family home to relatives and was not to rejoin her brother for nine years. This was a time "when prison gates [began] to close upon the growing child" (Wordsworth 1807, 589). A year later William was sent off to Hawkshead School. His father, John, died in 1783 when thirteen-year-old William was away at school. The boy felt guilty about his father's death. His father was the subservient, hardworking, mistreated yet well-paid local political agent of the politically powerful, unscrupulous, and hated Earl of Lonsdale (Lord Lowther). His agent drew rancor by treating people less powerful than himself "as their master treated [him]" (see Johnston 1998, 16). John Wordsworth was loyal to the earl; he was kept busy enough as his lordship's agent not to be able to pay much attention to his children after their mother's death.

Recovery

Fortunately the grammar school was a happy place for the boy. He called it "beloved Hawksworth" (Gill, 18). This was in large part because he lodged with Anne Tyler. Tyler and her husband became good substitute parents for the boy, and Wordsworth lived with the couple from 1779 to 1787 (ages nine to seventeen). He has paid wonderful tribute to Anne Tyler in his poetry.

The Poet as a Precursor of Psychoanalytic Ideas

Wordsworth can be (and has been) presented in the psychoanalytic literature as a proto-Freudian or a proto-Kleinian. He writes in "The Prelude" of "the eagerness of infantine desire"[5] (1805, 72), which can be taken to refer both to the intensity of instinctual drives and to the perfervid quality of the perceptions of early life. In the "Immortality Ode," Wordsworth (as Lionel Trilling [1948] points out)—in his references to celestial light, splendor in the grass, glory from the earth—is describing what Freud was to term the oceanic feeling of being at one with the universe that stems from the initial narcissistic period of infantile life. In "The Prelude," he looks back from age seventeen when he left his "Paradise" at Hawkshead for Cambridge and says of this period of his childhood,

> I, at this time,
> Saw blessings spread around me like a sea.

[5] "Ah, is there one who ever has been young, . . . /And is there one , the wisest and the best/Of all mankind, who does not sometimes wish/For things which cannot be; who would not give,/If so he might, to duty and to truth/The eagerness of infantine desire?" (1805, 72).

> Thus the days flew by, and years passed on,
> From Nature and her overflowing soul,
> I had received so much, that all my thoughts
> Were steeped in feeling; I was only then
> Contented, when with bliss ineffable
> I felt the sentiment of Being spread
> O'er all that moves and all that seemeth still;
> O'er all that, lost beyond the reach of thought
> And human knowledge, to the human eye
> Invisible, yet liveth in the heart (1805/1850, 95).

Wordsworth, well aware of the importance of the mother in the fashioning of the infant's and the adult's mind, wrote in "The Prelude,"

> Blest the infant Babe . . . who with his soul
> Drinks in the feelings of his mother's eye
>   (1805/1850, 85).

And adds,

> From early days,
> Beginning not long after that first time
> In which, a Babe, by intercourse of touch
> I held mute dialogs with my Mother's breast,[6]
> I have endeavoured to display the means
> Whereby *the infant sensibility*—

[6] Wordsworth "knows" that the infant's merger and separation begin at mother's breast. He anticipates here the importance of what psychoanalysts call mirroring—the baby's taking in and responding to the gleam of loving recognition in the mother's eye that fuels its psychic structure and function.

> Great birthright of our being, was in me
> Augmented and sustained. (87–88; emphasis
>   added)

The "infant sensibility," for good and for bad, is, whether augmented or reduced, sustained in all of us. But it can be inhibited or blocked, and we must be able to feel it to know it is there. Lionel Trilling, in his fine essay on Wordsworth (1950), writes that the poet repeatedly in his poems describes a very old, destitute, or defective human being. "And then suddenly, startlingly, in what we have learned to call an 'epiphany,' to show forth the intensity of his human existence" (193). Trilling quotes Matthew Arnold's comment, "In a wintry clime, in an iron time, Wordsworth taught us to *feel*" (191). Trilling adds, "Wordsworth did, or tried to do, more than make us feel: he undertook to teach us how to be. . . . It is an attractive thing about Wordsworth, and it should be a reassuring thing, that his *acute sense of the being of others derives from, and serves to affirm and heighten, his acute sense of his own being*. . . . Arnold [attributes] to Wordsworth a '*healing power*' through an ability to make us feel" (Trilling 1950, 192, 194; emphasis added). Knowing accompanied by feeling makes for the empathy that underlies caring and loving. The psychological therapist needs that "healing power through an ability to make [one] feel," to allow the patient to empathize both with self and other. I will restate this, changing the order in the quotations from Trilling. The patient must be able to attain—partly by virtue of the analyst's possessing and transmitting the "healing power that makes us feel"—the "acute sense of his own being" that "serves to affirm and heighten the acute sense of the being of others."[7]

[7] By recapturing in the course of the analysis something of what Wordworth calls "the infant sensibility" from the patient's early childhood and relationship with mother and father.

The healing power of the analyst or therapist or a loving other depends on the revival of the patient's feelings from the past that centered on the parents and then on parental figures being brought to life in relation to the "healer" in the present.[8] The evocation of the past (if the patient can allow it) can bring (I am quoting Wordsworth) "sweet tears." He was thinking of his beloved sister and lifelong companion, Dorothy, and of his foster mother, Anne Tyler, when he wrote,

> She gave me eyes; she gave me ears,
> And humble cares and delicate fears,
> A heart, the fountain of *sweet tears,*
> And love, and thought, and *joy.* (1801, 79;
>   emphasis added)

I repeat: Henrik Ibsen wrote that soul murder is the killing of the capacity for joy in another human being.

[8] The technical term for this in psychoanalytic theory is "transference."

V
Change Means Loss: Spring and Summer Must Become Winter

All things that we ordained festival,

Turn from their office to black funeral;

Our instruments to melancholy bells,

Our wedding cheer to a sad burial feast,

Our solemn hymns to sullen dirges change,

Our bridal flowers serve for a buried cor[p]se,

And all things change them to the contrary.

—*Shakespeare,* Romeo and Juliet, *IV, iv, 112–18*

Most of what I am stressing stems from the genetic point of view in psychoanalysis that emphasizes the significant influence of the beginnings of phenomena. Clinging to beginnings leads to my emphasizing one of the psychological truths or half-truths I have become so aware of in my resistant patients: the inherent human (conservative) tendency to resist change.[1]

Change Means Loss, A Terrible Expectation

Some but not all of the kind of resistant patients I am referring to were victims of soul murder, abused and deprived as children.[2] Others for different reasons were terrified of the losses their aggressive-laden impulses made them anticipate. Rage, no matter if we are born with it or it is developed in reaction to experience—it probably is both—can turn against the self and also against the parents; both directions are frightening, even traumatic, for the young child. Whether or not there had been significant abuse or neglect in childhood, these children terrified of anger are burdened as adults with unconscious and conscious terrible *expectations.*

In his paper on the Rat Man, Freud (1909) reports the Rat Man quoting to him from Nietzsche: "'I did this,' says my Memory. 'I cannot have done this,' says my Pride, and *remains inexorable.* In the end, Memory yields" (184; emphasis added). For soul murder victims, or those who are consciously or unconsciously preoccupied with accusing their parents of abuse that the parents may or may not have actually committed, the accusation toward the parent (potential memory or "mem-

---

[1] This conservative tendency is accompanied by an inherent conflicting one to achieve change.

[2] See Shengold 1989.

ory"?) is usually doubted or disowned.[3] (Sometimes this doubt exists alongside certainty of the justness of the accusation, in a kind of Orwellian "doublethink.") I am altering the quotation here: "'You [the parent or parent-figure] did this,' says my Memory. 'You cannot have done this,' says Need [rather than Pride] and *remains inexorable.* Memory, or at least the responsibility for making the accusation, yields."

Not Knowing

The "inexorable" push toward not knowing is fueled by the unbearable intensity of the child's conflicting feelings of need and of rage, the torture of the longing for and hatred toward parents without whom one once felt, and can continue to feel, one could not and cannot survive. With the regressive revivals in the transference onto the analyst of rage accompanied by terrifying expectations of loss, the resistance can indeed threaten to "remain inexorable."

Bad Expectations Evoked by Hope

The approach of every season evokes the prospect of change, of transformations that can be anticipated from past experience as mixtures of being for the better and for the worse. These expectations consist of the promise of pleasure, growth, and improvement as well as (the other side of the same coin) of pain, danger, and loss. The predominant quality of the mixture of such presentiments and feelings is conditioned for each individual by the current external realities as well as by conscious

---

[3] The person can also be projecting his or her own hostile and sexual wishes onto the parent or transferring hostility and sexual wishes toward someone else onto the parent.

and unconscious (frequently insistent) expectations derived from fantasies based on past experiences.[4] The neurotic expectations of the resistant patients I am describing are usually predominantly and often clamorously bad.

The Mixed Promise of Spring—A Specific Instance

Every year newspapers and magazines remind us of the promise of spring by quoting what have become poetic clichés: "April showers bring the flowers that bloom in May"; "fresh as is the month of May";[5] and "the darling buds of May."[6] But T. S. Eliot (1922) reminds us that "April is the cruelest month, breeding lilacs out of the dead land" (744). Hope for change *can* be cruel, specifically when change predominantly is expected to bring loss or even catastrophe (that is, when one anticipates with great anxiety any or all of Freud's (1926) universal developmental "danger-situations" that start to exist for us in childhood).[7]

Being Haunted by Parents

"The imagination of disaster" is a phrase of Henry James relevant to a characteristic of those who predominantly expect that change will mean loss.[8] Such an apprehension means

---

[4] The experience is not necessarily based on an actual happening—it can be the psychic reexperience of past fantasies.

[5] Chaucer, *The Canterbury Tales* (1385?). *Prologue*, line 92 (1385?).

[6] Shakespeare, *Sonnet 18*, line 3 (1593?).

[7] Traumatic overstimulation (ego dissolution), loss of the mother, loss of the mother's love, castration anxiety, fear of one's own conscience (superego).

[8] It was written in a letter of 1896: "But I have the imagination of disaster, and see life as ferocious and sinister" (quoted in Trilling 1948, 57). James, too, suffered much from bad expectations, which we all do to different degrees.

being haunted by the conviction (which may be unconscious or disavowed but sometimes is of almost delusional intensity) that what starts with promise (May, spring, garden, flowers) will end in catastrophe and death. This promise is experienced as stemming from the parents, and its presence as it continues (sometimes not in responsible consciousness) in later life is one manifestation of being haunted by parents. But why such bad expectations are there is not always determinable. I feel that their presence depends largely on individual vicissitudes of murderous impulses, directed toward the self or toward important others. Hate-filled intensities can come into being both from what one is born with and from the inevitable traumata and frustrations one has experienced.[9]

Quasi-delusional bad expectations are almost always found in people who have actually suffered sexual abuse, beatings, and emotional and physical deprivation as children;[10] of course they can *also* be found in those who suffer from sadomasochistic fantasy that has not necessarily been induced by traumatic or deprivatory experience.

Children who have been traumatized tend to sexualize abuse even if the trauma has not been overtly sexual. The need for love and the sexual promise of pleasure (often disguising the urgent necessity of escaping from concurrent frustration,

[9] For Freud, what is inherited as part of human nature would feature the instinctual drives, sex and aggression, and also some inherent deficiencies and variations in defenses against those drives.

[10] Primo Levi (1987) reminds us that, once tortured, one can never again feel secure in the world. The implication is that once one has been in a concentration camp, physical liberation doesn't mean psychological liberation. This applies to the soul murder victims of family concentration camps. And of course there are school concentration camps, as readers of Charlotte Brontë's *Jane Eyre* know (see also Rebecca Fraser's biography of Charlotte Brontë [1988, 38–42]).

danger, and pain) are what originally led the child-victim to open up, physically and emotionally, to the adult—frequently the parent—only to experience traumatic overstimulation and inevitable frustration.[11] The insistent need for repetition—accompanied by the delusion that the next instance will end in pleasure—becomes part of a compulsion to repeat what the traumatized child cannot bear to reexperience. And, in the course of this dynamically charged, conflict ridden double bind or no-win situation—wanting what one dreads and dreading what one wants—the need for love and the prospect of pleasure can become as or more frightening than the prospect of pain. Change, perhaps especially in the direction of pleasure, has come to mean unbearable expectations that threaten loss.

Negative Therapeutic Reaction and the Compulsion to Repeat

One observes in these patients variously manifest expressions of the sequence of a desperate plea, "Help me!"—followed by an angry "I won't let you help me!" This contradictory mental set involves a tendency toward paradoxical negative reactions to pleasure and success. Realistic achievements, inner satisfactions, and the feeling of power call forth self-deprecating and self-destructive feelings and actions. The needs for punishment, for failure, and for illness become subject to a compulsion to repeat traumatic situations, resulting in tendencies to hurt others as well as oneself; the compulsion to repeat is at the heart of some of the most illogical but powerful ingredients of neurotic motivation. (Of course all these tendencies exist in nonpatients as well.)

[11] Children do not have adequate ways to discharge overexcitement or intense sexual arousal.

There is a basic source of the theme of this book in a description by Freud (1937) of the developmentally inevitable human burden of aggression that becomes partially directed inwardly toward the self.[12] What results are individual versions of "the sense of guilt and the need for punishment" (242) that result in phenomena associated with masochistic motivation that make for resistances in psychoanalytic treatment and, more fundamentally—I am sure Freud would agree—to resistances to change for the better in life: "No stronger impression arises from the *resistance* during the work of analysis than there being a force which is defending [the self] by every possible means against recovery and which is absolutely resolved to hold on to illness and suffering" (242; emphasis added).[13]

The Sadomasochistic Tie to the Parents and the Past

A strong investment in masochistic motivation makes for sadomasochistic feeling, fantasy, and action that can be characterologic—that is, can involve an individual's entire character. Sadomasochism is unconsciously used as a way of psychologically holding on to the past and to a sense of belonging to the parents of the past—another aspect of being haunted by parents. As Freud demonstrates in "A Child Is Being Beaten" (1919), there are children who, in order to maintain some central importance to the parent, cultivate physical punishment, humilia-

---

[12] I am indebted to Dr. Rosemary Balsam for pointing out to me these passages from Freud's "Analysis, Terminable and Interminable."

[13] Freud goes on to say that the need for punishment, suffering, and failure leads to our "no longer being able to adhere to the belief that mental events are exclusively governed by the desire for pleasure" (243). Part of our nature exists beyond the pleasure principle and features the need to repeat traumatic events.

tion, and failure—to be hated or hurt, frightening as these can be, is better than parental indifference or absence. In order for the sadomasochistic hate-filled tie to be tolerated and maintained, it has to be idealized or sexualized sufficiently to diminish or neutralize the dangerous intensity of the involved aggression. The child feels that its murderous impulses have the power of magical wishes that can kill the indispensable parents. I want to emphasize that for the small child, immersed in magical thinking, simply *feeling* murderously intense rage means possessing the power to destroy; this is terrifying. The terror can be overwhelming and become traumatic when it is directed toward godlike parents without whom one cannot live, who are suddenly felt to have lost their divinity and become vulnerable. Loss of the parent is one consequent unbearable expectation; the fear of the parent's ability to retaliate and kill the child is another. The danger of a killing rage directed at mother and father can continue for the adult, consciously or unconsciously, both toward the actual parents and toward the parents present in the mind. (It is these parental "imagos" that continue to haunt the adult.)

Ghosts

The unconscious mental registrations of the parents form and, alongside their maturation and transformation in the course of development, *remain* part of the content and structure of our minds. If these parental "ghosts" are predominantly or more than transiently hostile and/or vulnerable, the revival of the childhood terrible expectations can amount to a feeling (frequently only latently present in the conscious part of the mind) of being obsessed with, or even possessed by, parents. Whenever such regressive feelings are intense, there is inhibition or attenuation of caring for people other than the parents and of caring about issues not associated with them. This haunting can be disguised if someone else has unconsciously been assigned a parental role—as the analyst will be in course of the intense regressive transference feelings aroused by an analysis that works. These can then be dealt with in the analysis as they are brought into responsible consciousness.

Rage in relation to the parents means fear for them and fear of them. The early parents (especially the initial mothering person, the primal parent) are associated with omnipotence and magic. The black magic is destructive and terrifying. The positive magic is full of grandiose promise: Wordsworth's "clouds of glory." This initial narcissistic magic, which begins with a feeling of being merged with an omnipotent parent, must inevitably dwindle and fade, a loss that means for all of us an expulsion from the Garden of Eden. The child is destined to bring the need for magical deliverance—from evil and death, from the burdens and dangers of life, from the indifference and cruelties of fate—to the parental gods. Whenever they are felt to be malign gods, the dependent child can nevertheless usually turn only to them for rescue. But the rescue does not or cannot occur if and when the parenting has been really consistently bad—or if the child is born with significant deficiencies to be unable to profit from good parental care, or (worst of all) has suffered traumatic loss of parenting. Such ill-used or unfortunate children are left with the insistent need for a delusion of rescue—often by way of a compulsive idealized sadomasochistic attachment. There is an unconscious insistence that the next time, the next contact, with the bad parental figure (to be magically transformed to good in cruel repetitious anticipations) will reverse the pattern, fulfill the promise of liberation, take away the dangers of killing and being killed, and provide a return to Paradise. The child is left in a trap of conflicting emotions, craving and fearing, seeking and avoiding change at the hands of parents. In this sense some live all their lives with, and we can all under conditions inducing regression be reduced to, the terrible conflicts within the minds of those children and former children condemned to assume and even to insist that there is no life without mother and father. Of course such solutions are maladaptive and belong to that psychic realm where pain and loss are being unconsciously sought—a realm that contains illogical destructive and self-destructive motivations that Freud (1920) characterizes as existing "beyond the pleasure principle."

Sadomasochism and Repetition Compulsion

Sadomasochism, both as a perverse part of sexuality and as sadomasochistic character structure, can provide gratification and reassurance as well as anxiety. Both modes also can represent identification with (= becoming like) the parent, alongside a repetition of submissive and/or defiant relationship with the parent that held, and can still hold in the present, promise of a desperately needed happy resolution that never occurs.

There is, in the adult, a compulsion to repeat and hold onto the original or replacement relationships. (Freud suggests that part of the explanation of the need to repeat traumatic events is the expectation that the next repetition will have a happy resolution; I see that expectation as a kind of delusional promise, usually unconscious but with great power to motivate actions.)[14] The contact with the sadistic parent who must

---

[14] See chapter 14.

not be lost, or with the person who currently plays that role (as the analyst inevitably will), is stubbornly held onto out of desperate need. The promise that the parents will rescue, and the need not to accept their inability to do so, is a cruel part of the haunting. The parental figure in one's mind plays the role of a beckoning "good" ghost whose blandishments, if accepted, will lead to destructive loss of individuality or worse.

Revenge

One of the developmental vicissitudes of murderous aggression, whether regarded as inborn instinct or inevitable reaction to frustration, is a motivational drive for revenge. This begins, like everything else, in relation to parents. The revenge is the infant's (initially unconscious) reaction directed to the continuing and burgeoning betrayal by the primal parent, whose promise of the child being and having everything begins its inevitable diminishment. The guilt-ridden accusatory feeling that accompanies this developmental course can be expressed as directed toward the parental gods as, "Look what you have done to me!" (Compare Christ's reproach on the cross—from the gospel of St. Matthew: "My God, my God, wherefore hast thou forsaken me?") Such rebukes and the urge for vengeance will be revived in relation to the therapist or analyst. What is there to be felt is something like, "I want to get rid of you. You deserve it!" This powerful murderous wish results in an unbearable mixture of guilt toward, and a terror of loss of, the indispensable parent. The promise of everything has become the fear of change.[15]

[15] Patients whom I have seen who have been or think they have been soul-murdered are beset by an excess of sadomasochistic impulse and action. The motivating push for revenge in these people was mainly expressed

Clinging to Bad Parental Figures

The paradoxical clinging to bad parenting (in this case to bad parental substitutes after a child's loss of his good parents) is illustrated in Oliver Sacks's wonderful memoir *Uncle Tungsten* (2001). Sacks writes of his having been sent out, as a child of five, of his parental home in London during the blitz to attend a boarding school (Braefield). It was badly run, and for him it was a living nightmare of being neglected, ill-fed, and repeatedly beaten by his sadistic headmaster and (perhaps worst of all) of despair that his parents had abandoned him. After four years of hellish exile (about which he never complained to his parents), he was sent to a well-run school (St. Lawrence College), where he was not mistreated. But his reaction to this fortunate change was full of loneliness and terror. He missed the place of persecution that had been his home for four years: "I think my sense of isolation, of being uncared for and unknown, may have been even greater at St. Lawrence than it was at Braefield, where even the sadistic attentions of the headmaster could be seen as a sort of concern, even love" (30).

---

masochistically in the form of identification with the aggressor. That is, the parents were spared, but sadism and revenge were aimed (in impulse and action) for the most part at the self and at children who stand for self as child. The essence of masochism can be found by compounding two maxims: (1) the distortion of a cliché by the late nineteenth-century writer Samuel Butler: "'Tis better to have loved and lost than never to have *lost* at all" (emphasis added); (2) from the great early nineteenth-century poet William Blake: "The cut worm forgives the plough." The latter maxim brings in the "worm's" identification with the aggressor. I feel sure that there are countless individual variations in how developmental aggression is manifested. Certainly hatred and wish for revenge in relation to the parental or other adult aggressors have been predominant in many who have been able to maintain rage that can be expressed in sadistic or murderous action. Most murderers end up in jail, not in analysis.

Garden Time in the Transference

I mentioned in my discussion of patient X that in mid-May, during lilac time—as Memorial Day, summer, the Fourth of July, and the traditional August analytic vacation loom or beckon—it is my custom to remind patients of the forthcoming holidays in conjunction with announcing the dates of the August hiatus.[16] This of course brings a prospect of separation and the danger of desertion by the parents into the transference of the past onto the analyst in the present. For those brought up in America, the danger is reinforced by the holiday of Memorial Day, usually not consciously associated with evoking much emotion but becoming important for some partly because of its place in the calendar. The late spring holiday often is the unconscious harbinger of past and future changes. Spring marks the approach of summer with its long sunny days and the full bloom of gardens. Summer also connotes the separations involved in graduations and weddings, the passing of the school year, going to camp, parental vacations with and away from the child. Also (in America), Memorial Day arrives between the celebrations of Mother's Day in mid-May and Father's Day in June. These commercially driven but, for children and even ex-children, potentially emotion-laden holidays are meant to celebrate the living parent or the one who may be dead or absent. But also these parental "Days" evoke the memory of the centrality of the parent of earlier and earliest times. I have long noticed that for many patients Memorial Day seems to function as an unconscious injunction to remember— to remember the past, especially the traumatic past. Loss is emphasized, directing one's memory to the dead and therefore

---

[16] For analysands, August is the cruelest month.

to death and the loss of childhood and its intimations of immortality—glory and the gleam of celestial light.[17]

Change Means Loss

So, for patients in psychoanalysis or in any psychological treatments where transference of emotions toward figures from the past is evoked, worked with, and flourishes, the promise and especially the bad expectations of spring and of summer gardens can, if the treatment "takes," inevitably become connected with the analyst's vacation.[18] The ghosts of the parents and parental figures from the past and the intense feelings connected with them are revived and transferred onto the analyst in the present. To use Freud's simile, the revival in the transference provides the taste of blood of the living that awakens ghosts to new life, "like the ghosts of the underworld in the *Odyssey*" (1900, 553). (Only then, Freud implies, when their presence is palpably felt and owned in relation to the analyst, can the *revenants* be exorcised or robbed of their power.) The revived intense emotions feature the bad or even terrible expectations of the danger-situations experienced in earlier and earliest life threatening separation from and loss of the parents.

Some of this equation of change with loss is inevitable in human development, as Wordsworth's great "Immortality Ode" reminds us. Sometimes, the bad expectations that begin to come to life again in relation to the analyst were of traumatic intensity. Sometimes, but not always, these traumatic experiences of loss turned out to be in large part the products of fan-

[17] The holiday functions as a kind of *memento mori*.

[18] Patients' lip service to good expectations of the vacation are sometimes voiced, and even when genuinely felt and not hollow, this is almost always also in the service of defensive distancing of bad, hate-filled feelings.

tasy, but for many they had been actually lived out in reality. (If so, this must become manifest in the course of the treatment and not be assumed beforehand.)

The (at least) unconscious injunction to remember and honor the parent evoked by changes in the seasons and their associated customs and holidays provides material for powerful metaphors that can denote and also be elicited by developmental changes. These changes call forth conscious and unconscious mental conflicts about separation from the parents and achieving one's own identity; they can have considerable motivational force. Resistance to the changes felt as likely to bring about loss of a parent can be expressed by compliant submission to parental authority, compulsive rebellion (which amounts to negative compliance), or by a mixture of both.

The almost inevitable evocation of change meaning loss is part of the ever-present psychic tendency to connect the past[19] with the present—what in psychoanalysis is termed the metapsychological genetic point of view. In this book I am focusing on the genetic view of what psychoanalysts call object relations. This is an unfortunately clumsy term for the development of the meaningfulness of others. That development, beginning with psychic merger with and then separating from the parent, goes on toward the attainment of an individual identity—a sense of a separate self—and a concomitant feeling of the importance of being related to other people. This progression is a pathway full of conflicts, regressions, and transformations.

[19] Here the past is idealized; it of course can also be devalued, and both can be present in all sorts of mixtures, including more or less appropriate and realistic ones.

VI
The Myth of Demeter
and Persephone

She waits for each and other,
  She waits for all men born;
Forgets the earth her mother,
  The life of fruits and corn,
And spring and seed and swallow
Take wing for her and follow
Where summer song is hollow
  And flowers are put to scorn.
—*A. C. Swinburne, "The Garden of Proserpine"**

*Proserpine is Latin for Persephone.

The promise of spring and summer is of course of much deeper significance and of more ancient origin than the cultural events involved in customs and holidays currently associated with the prospect of the warm seasons. Harvest festivals and sacrifices marking the end of summer and the approach of autumn come from ancient times and are part of the stuff of myths. The well-known Greek myth of Demeter and Persephone alludes to the change of seasons; it also exemplifies the link between change and expectation of loss and emphasizes the myth's psychological origin in the developmental separation from mother.[1] Demeter was the daughter of the Greek Ur-Gods Cronus and Rhea and therefore the sister of Zeus. (The Romans called her Ceres, and her daughter Persephone, Proserpine.) Demeter was the goddess of corn and harvests, and she was celebrated at harvest time by a festival. In early Greece, it was woman's work to till and harvest the grain. Part of the festival eventually became secret and developed into the famous Eleusinian mysteries. (These "civilized" celebratory festivals had developed from historically earlier cruel and even murderous harvest rituals that had involved human sacrifice.)

Demeter's male counterpart was her brother Dionysus (Roman name: Bacchus), god of wine. His worship also involved sacrifice and murder. The Maenads or Bacchantes or Bacchae were female worshipers of Dionysus, who in their rituals became crazed with wine. In myth and tragedies, Orpheus was torn to pieces in their frenzied rage, and (in Euripides' myth-derived play *The Bacchae)* they murdered King Pentheus, who spied on their forbidden ceremonies.

[1] An example of the genetic point of view.

Demeter, in contrast, was connected mainly with benevolence, but both she and Dionysus, the two earth deities associated with bread and wine, could be cruel as well. They can represent ambivalently regarded primal parent figures—the omnipotent and omniscient early parents unconsciously transformed in religion, myth, and literature into gods.

Demeter had a daughter, Persephone, the goddess of spring. Persephone was the child of an incestuous union—her father was Demeter's brother, Zeus.[2] An early Homeric hymn (from about 800 BC) is the first written record that tells the familiar story of the relationship between the mother and her only child. Persephone was stolen away from her mother by Pluto, the god of the underworld, to be his wife. Demeter heard her daughter's cry when she was abducted. In her loneliness and mourning for Persephone, Demeter withheld her gifts and blessings of the earth so that nothing grew. As a Victorian poet put it,

> Demeter:
> My quick tears kill'd the flower, my ravings hush'd
> The bird, and lost in utter grief I fail'd
> To send my life thro' olive-yard and vine
> And golden-grain, my gift to helpless man,
> Rain-rotten died; the wheat, the barley spears
> Were hollow-husk'd, the leaf fell, and the Sun,
> Pale at my grief, drew down before his time
> Sickening, and Aetna kept her winter snow.
> (Tennyson 1889, 846)

---

[2] Incest being the privilege of the Gods in Greek (and other, e.g., Egyptian) myth.

The resultant misery of human beings and the threat that they would all die of starvation in their perpetual winter induced Zeus to send Hermes to Hades to restore Persephone to her mother. ("Is there life without mother?") Pluto knew he had to cede to his brother Zeus's will, but he forced Persephone to eat a pomegranate seed that would make her return to him four months each year. These four months thenceforth marked the winter season during which Persephone returned to Hades, the place of the dead; and during that time no plants grew on earth. The other seasons were restored. Edith Hamilton (1940) writes, "Demeter, goddess of the harvest wealth, was still more the divine sorrowing mother who saw her daughter die each year. Persephone was the radiant maiden of the spring and the summertime, whose light step upon the dry, brown hillside was enough to make it fresh and blooming. But all the while Persephone knew how brief that beauty was; fruits, flowers, leaves, all the growth of earth, must end with the coming of the cold and pass like herself into the power of death" (53–54). So, in the myth spring means change as a coming to life and a return to mother—followed by separation from the mother, loss, and death. Persephone was torn between Pluto and Demeter.

Good expectations are evoked by Percy Bysshe Shelley's (1819) well-known line "If Winter comes, can Spring be far behind?" (752).[3] The poet is expressing good expectations that can lighten a time of storm and strife. Our minds also contain the bad expectations I have been stressing that can emerge if one reverses the time sequence: "If Spring comes, can Winter be far behind?"

The earliest extant literary version of the Demeter/

[3] In his "Ode to the West Wind" (1819).

Persephone story is from the Homeric Hymns—the date of their creation is not known. The usual guess is c. 800–600 BC, long after *The Iliad* and *The Odyssey* (c. 1200–750 BC?), perhaps about the time of, but not by, Hesiod (c. 800–750 BC). The extant fragment reads as follows (a shortened version of the prose translation I am quoting from has been called "Persephone Snatched Away"):

> I sing of fair-haired Demeter, the venerable goddess, and her slender-ankled daughter, whom the king of Hades snatched away, and who was given to him by all-watching Zeus, as she was playing far from gold-sworded Demeter, the giver of splendid fruit. She was gathering flowers in a lush meadow—the rose, the crocus, beautiful violets and irises and the hyacinth—and a narcissus which the Earth had grown to deceive the blushing girl and so please the king of Hades, according to the wishes of Zeus. It sparkled marvelously, a wonder to all who saw it whether immortal gods or mortal men. From its root had grown a hundred blossoms, and it had the sweetest perfume, and the wide sky above, the earth and the salty swell of the sea smiled [in reflection of it]. And Persephone was amazed and stretched out her hands to take hold of the beautiful toy; but the wide-pathed earth yawned, and [Hades], the king who receives all, leapt up with his immortal horses. Against her will he seized her and took her away weeping on his golden chariot. She cried out, calling shrilly on her father, [Zeus], the first and best of the gods. But no god or mortal man heard her voice. (Homeric Hymn, c. 800–600 BC?, 118–19)

Here the false promise of the flowers of spring gives rise to the fulfillment of the worst expectations from childhood of mother and daughter—separation and loss.[4]

The presence of good and bad expectations can exist in individual variations. In the cycle dealt with in the myth of Persephone and Demeter, the bad alternates with the good. Everyone has some kind of dynamically changeable mixture of bad-and-good. For peace of mind, an easy restoration of optimal balance is needed.

In old age, many go back to a second childhood and want or demand maternal care (for example, King Lear). And sometimes the wish or need for a parent returns when death approaches. A few days after Leo Tolstoy had run away from his wife and family, he collapsed. The old man is said to have cried out in his delirium, several days before he died, "Mama, hold me, baby me!"[5]

---

[4] The centrality of the narcissus flower in this version of the myth can stand for the inevitable shrinking (loss) of narcissism and narcissistic promise ("I am the center of the world").

[5] I do not remember what book I read this in, but I am sure I did read it.

VII

Another Dream of Death in a Garden

All are at one now, roses and lovers,
  Not known of the cliffs and the fields and the sea.
Not a breath of the time that has been hovers
  In the air now soft with a summer to be.
Not a breath shall there sweeten the seasons hereafter
  Of the flowers or the lovers that laugh now or weep,
When as they that are free now of weeping and
  laughter
  We shall sleep.
—A. C. Swinburne, "A Forsaken Garden"

A woman, Y, in her early forties, who had a successful career and had achieved a fairly satisfactory marriage after years of psychoanalysis in another part of the country, returned to analysis shortly after moving to New York. She felt conflicted about her husband's wish to have a child and depressed about the stalemate in her professional role in a very competitive field. Y still felt the need to provoke failure.

After years of her second analysis with me, there had been very little change. She had given up on her attempt to get pregnant, which she had described as "halfhearted at best." She was an only child and had suffered from the intense kind of sibling rivalry—never lived out and, therefore, as often happens when there are no siblings or significant sibling-figures to react to and with, never sufficiently worked out and attenuated—that can exist for only children. Although Y was aware she was valued in her work for her considerable talents, she still felt inadequate. She consistently provoked her superiors and resisted or spoiled opportunities to advance or to become more independent. Her work was respected, but she was not liked. Y was working in her father's field and jokingly said she had learned from reading Freud that she had trouble being more successful than her father. But this was not a joking matter. She had been her father's *confidante* in her childhood and youth, but, although proud of her academic achievements, he had subsequently discouraged her ambition, first to go to college and, after she got through on scholarships, to continue on to graduate work.

Y resisted acknowledging and working with her feelings about me, and so (despite my interpretive attempts) these remained largely unconnected with her intense ambivalent attachments to her parents, who had died when she was in her early thirties. Interpretations of transference and the resistances to transference were accepted intellectually but, she claimed, never felt; yet her longing to be loved by and her anger toward me were obvious but not owned. She frequently attributed to me (as a male) negatively critical opinions and beliefs about women. These views were based on semidelusional "convictions" about what I "really" must be thinking and doing that were in accord with her own version of what she called her feminist views about men.

In the analysis, Y often displayed an insistence that I disapproved of everything about her, and she tried insistently to provoke reproach and punishment. These manifestly negative transference feelings were also denied and therefore disowned by her. She claimed she felt indifferent about me (this was proclaimed in an angry tone), yet would state that although she knew "in a way" that she *was* trying to provoke me, "I just don't accept that." She did get upset whenever I would go away, yet this too was verbally admitted but essentially disavowed. She mentioned her distress at being sent to summer camp as a child but then went on to insist that she, "if anything," looked forward to my being away.

Death in the Garden

Y started her treatment a few years after X had finished his analysis, but she had a dream whose manifest details and evocative circumstances so resembled his that I began to think of writing and publishing a brief communication about both dreams. Y, like X, also had her dream toward the end of May, following my telling her about forthcoming holidays and the dates of my August vacation, and it too was a dream about Death in a garden. Like her emotionally distant but domineer-

ing mother, Y was passionately fond of gardens. The dream
had started off beautifully, she said, full of color and promise.[1]
Y was passively watching her mother weeding her flowerbeds.
Her mother had seemed so happy doing it. But then, although
she couldn't recall the details, she became aware that somehow
Death was in the garden. It had not been a nightmare, but Y
woke in mild anxiety.

The anniversary of her parents' death was approaching.
They had been killed in an automobile crash. It was ironic that
her mother, the lover of gardens, had died in an accident when
on vacation in a desert. Y quoted the once-familiar lines, "We
are nearer God's heart in a garden / Than anywhere else on
earth" but wryly added, "What kind of a God lets accidents like
that happen?"[2]

Y associated to the Garden of Eden and the tree of knowledge; the forbidden fruit; the unfairness of blaming the expulsion and the beginning of mortality on Eve. God preferred
boys and men, as had her father. But father had at first treated
his only child like a boy and had always discouraged her from
helping mother in the garden. He called it "sissy-work." Her father had left home when Y was an adolescent but reappeared
after several years, and the parents reconciled. During his absence Y had started to work with her mother in the garden. She
enjoyed it and continued to help her mother even after her father returned. Now Y loved gardens, but she also "realized" she
hated them. That's how she had felt toward her controlling
mother and her deserting father too. She had no such ambiva-

[1] I feel that dreams that are consciously described as involving color
usually involve the body. I heard Robert Fliess once say he had heard this
from Freud in a conversation, but I have not found it in Freud's publications.

[2] From the poem "The Lord God Planted a Garden" by Dorothy
Frances Gurney (1913, 6–7).

lence about cut flowers and kept criticizing me for not having fresh flowers in my office. Arranging flowers gave her great pleasure; part of this (I felt) was pleasure at the feeling of control. She had, as part of her "feminist" prejudices, a particular dislike for male gardeners. She told me she was aware "it was neurotic to feel that."

A typical negation followed her narrating her dream: "I *know* you will say I had this dream because you told me you are going away, but that is *not* what *I* feel!" This was said with considerable emotion. I pointed out what sounded like the angry emphasis of her disclaimer but to little effect. (It took years for her to own the feelings connecting past with present that underlay the conflicts alluded to in this dream—the despair at the threat of separation and loss, and yet the rage that accompanied wanting to get rid of her parents and have different ones.)

Y went on in her associations to gardens to cite Genesis further, pointing out in relation to the dream that both human life and murder had begun only after the expulsion from Eden. In retrospect, the dream marked a turning point in her analysis. She made subsequent use of it in her slow but finally successful struggle to acknowledge and work with her deeply ambivalent feelings toward me.

She eventually became able to tolerate her powerfully conflicted emotions. I felt, as Y grudgingly put it, that her analysis "*seemed* to be coming to" a successful conclusion, but I have not heard further from her since her leaving it. This is not at all a bad portent. Y's ambivalence was certainly still present. She did give me permission to write about her.

The analyst should not expect expressions of gratitude after the analysis. They sometimes occur, and it would always be pleasant and useful to hear what happened in the years that follow termination of the treatment. But one cannot count on either grateful (or ungrateful) sentiments being communicated, any more than we can feel entitled to such communication from our children. Of course, with one's children one can, if necessary, talk with them about it. But in relation to a former analytic patient, who needs to be allowed to process and integrate the analysis on her or his own, the analyst should be abstinent and contain his curiosity. Such restraint is easier to exercise if one reminds oneself that change, however positive, will also mean loss.

VIII
A Clinical and
a Literary Example—
Edna St. Vincent Millay

*Nothing in the world can touch the soul with such sadness as
the sight of portraits of beautiful women who have been dead
several hundred years. Melancholy steals over us at the thought
that nothing remains of their originals, of all those beauties
that were so charming, so coquettish, so witty, so roguish, so
capricious.* Of all those May-day heads with their April
humors, of all that maiden springtime—*nothing remains
but these multicolored shadows which a painter, like them
long since mouldered away, has painted on a perishable bit
of canvas, which is likewise crumbling with age.*
—*Heinrich Heine, "On portraits of beautiful women in a
Genoese Picture Gallery" [1830?] [emphasis added]*

Spring and summer give way to fall and winter; life ends in
death: change is loss.

Patient Z

Patient Z, seen many years ago, had been psychologically tied
to a cruel, paranoid father. He seemed bogged down in a long
analysis after an early surge of progress. Z was finally again beginning to feel responsible and to deal with his rage against,
and his longing for, me. Just before going away on an arbitrarily timed vacation (a bit of acting out in the analysis), he had a
dream. He was a child in a garden, and his father was beating
him on his bare buttocks with a strap. He was crouching, and
when struck, his back and buttocks oozed fluid that fell pro-
fusely in drops like *rain*, forming a pool in which small crabs
were swimming. Z said, "I felt as if anyone touched *it*, they
would get cancer."[1] He awoke in terror.

Z's dream from the distant past led me to think of a poem
of Edna St. Vincent Millay's entitled "Scrub" (1923), which had
been sent to me by the psychoanalyst Bonnie Asnes. She had
been reading one of my *Soul Murder* books and felt that Millay's poem expressed a cry from someone who knew what it
was to have been cruelly used in childhood. The poem uses the
metaphor of nourishing rain that has become mutilatingly
destructive:[2]

[1] The "it" here is ambiguous. Did the patient mean the pool or his behind? Z had been anally overstimulated as a child and had deep fears and
conflicts relating to his behind.

[2] In *The Merchant of Venice*, Portia uses the metaphor of rain to try to
douse Shylock's burning murderous and cannibalistic demand for a pound
of Antonio's flesh: "The quality of mercy is not strained./It droppeth as the
gentle *rain* from heaven/*Upon the place beneath*" (Shakespeare 1596, IV, i,
146–48; emphasis added). She of course pleads in vain to the ill-used man,

Scrub[3]
If I grow bitterly,
Like a gnarled and stunted tree,
Bearing harshly of my youth
Puckered fruit that sears the mouth;
[[This is fruit that burns and wounds.]]
If I make of my drawn boughs
An inhospitable house,
Out of which I never pry
Toward the water and the sky,
Under which I stand and hide
And hear the day go by outside;
It is that a wind too strong
Bent my back when I was young,
It is that I fear the *rain*
Lest it blister me again. (1923, 160; emphasis
   added)

The child/tree has been mutilated; the apple from the tree
of knowledge in the Garden of Eden of childhood has become
poisoned, the wind is injurious; mother's milk has turned to
acid rain.[4]

---

who craves revenge. Also from Eliot, following "April is the cruelest month:/
breeding lilacs out of the dead land," is "Mixing memory and desire,/Stirring
dull roots with spring *rain*" (1922, 744).

[3] Scrub—in the sense of a stunted tree.

[4] In contrast, from Millay's poem "Renascence," in which her rebirth is
to be accomplished by the benevolent rain: "The rain, I said, is kind to
come/And speak to me in my new home./I would I were alive again/To kiss
the fingers of the rain./Upset each cloud's gigantic gourd/And let the heavy
rain, down-poured/In one big torrent set me free,/Washing my grave away
from me! (1912, 6–7)—cf. the excerpt from her mother's diary that follows.

Edna St. Vincent Millay, Rain, and Gardens

There is an entry from the diary of Millay's mother, Cora, that links rain in summer with her three young daughters' delight in the tall grasses outside their home in Maine, nudity, and physical pleasure from the bodily contact of their mother's touch. It is a happy linkage: "There was nothing the girls so much liked as stripping, and putting on thin print dresses and running out into the summer grass and leaping about in the rain, letting the summer showers soak them until it ran in little rivers from their hair and faces. Then they came in and stripped and I rubbed them down with a rough Turkish towel till they glowed and tingled amid their laughter" (quoted by Epstein 2001, 9). Cora describes a scene of innocence and joy in the refreshing rain that evokes the Garden of Eden of child-hood before the Fall. After the expulsion from paradise comes the danger of blistering rain.

The garden—literary symbol of Mother Earth and of Gaea, the Earth Goddess and *Ur-Mutter* and Freudian symbol of Mother, her genitals and womb—is the place of safety and of danger, of the protected fetus and its expulsion from the body, of birth and of burial. The symbolism is especially rele-vant to enclosed gardens.[5]

Whether the author herself can be called a victim of soul

[5] There is additional symbolic resonance in the Garden of Eden as an enclosed space, as it was frequently depicted in ancient Roman and medieval painting—see "Garden of Paradise" by "Upper Rhenish Master" (1410) in the Frankfurt Stadelsche Kunstinstitut. The Garden of Eden is frequently pic-tured in medieval manuscripts as being closed. Medieval gardens tended to be *enclosed* gardens, as were many early Roman ones. For another closed gar-den, see the pertinent excerpt from Leonard Woolf's biography in the next chapter.

murder is not clear from her biographies. Two fascinating recent books about the poet by Nancy Milford (2001) and Daniel Epstein (2001) supply details and documentation that reveal how chaotic and disturbed and yet, intermittently, how happy her early life was. She had a lifelong intense attachment to her mother and a lifelong yearning for a father from whom she would not be separated, as she was from her real father for most of her life. This yearning was mostly unacknowledged consciously and made for actions directed toward father figures in some of the more lasting of her many love affairs. Millay wanted to have and wanted to be both parents.

Edna Vincent Millay was born in 1892 (she added the "St." later herself). She was born with a caul, traditionally believed to be a sign of the *promise* of good fortune. Her parents separated in 1900, when Millay was seven, and were divorced when she was nine. Cora Millay had had three daughters within her first four years of marriage to a charming but rather feckless man—a frequent gambler who usually lost and who could not keep a job to support the family adequately. Early in the marriage, Cora had fallen in love with the local minister. It is not clear whether the two became lovers. But she sent her husband, Henry, away.[6] After the parents' subsequent divorce, Henry married again and had a second family. He only occasionally obeyed the court's order to support his first three children. He is not mentioned in Edna's early diaries.

---

[6] There was a repetition here of Cora's mother Clementine's marriage. Clementine, after having six children by the time she was thirty-three (the age Cora dismissed Henry), fell in love with her doctor (also her sister's brother-in-law). She then followed *her* oldest daughter (then aged sixteen!) Cora's advice and left her husband. Cora intended to stay with her father and her two younger brothers (see Milford 2001). Unconventionality spanned the generations.

The mother, emotionally strong and determined, was at first indigent and dependent on friends and distant relatives. The little family had to move frequently. Cora supported herself and the girls by doing hairdressing, and then—finally settled at Camden, Maine—by nursing sick people at their homes. As a nurse she had to spend a good part of the time away from her daughters, occasionally out of town—and sometimes for weeks on end. (Milford writes that the mother was for long periods absent almost all the time.) When away, she kept in almost daily contact by writing to her daughters, and they wrote back to her. In case of emergencies, they could call on Cora Millay's aunt, who ran a boardinghouse close to their home. Apparently they seldom did.

Despite Cora's being away so much, the girls knew she cared about them intensely. She inspired them to follow her ardent artistic interests, and all three became adept at writing, painting, playing (and even composing) music, and acting. But most of the responsibility for cooking, cleaning, and keeping the household going fell to the little girls, especially to Vincent (as Edna was called), who was the eldest child—as her mother had been.[7] During Cora's frequent absences, Edna became the mother. Cora and daughters lived in rundown houses in poor neighborhoods in small towns in Maine and were always worried about not having enough money for food and rent. Only the mother's fervid determination and hard work (qualities she passed on to Edna) kept them going. She managed to supply necessities and even occasional luxuries (books, gifts) but could do so only by spending much time away from home. And the

[7] The masculine middle name (its habitual use must have contributed to Edna's confusion about her sexual identity) was supplied by Cora because, she said, of her gratitude to St. Vincent's Hospital in New York City for their good care of her brother Charles after he had a life-threatening accident.

houses were cold and drafty. Cora and the girls were often ill.
Edna would catch cold almost every month. Vincent's father occasionally sent gifts of a few dollars for his daughters, always promising more soon, but more almost never arrived. He continued to write letters to Edna (all of his letters to the family were addressed to her) full of apologies, always postponing his proposed visits. The only mention of an actual visit in Millay's letters concerns the one time, a little over a year after the separation, when he obeyed a summons from Cora commanding his return. The three little girls (aged nine, eight, and five) had come down with typhoid fever, caught after the mother had nursed some typhoid victims. At first they were not expected to live. Cora was beside herself with desperation, and apparently her letter to Henry held out some promise of reconciliation. After the girls' recovery began, Henry Millay, on Cora's refusal to take him back, did not stay long—and he never came back again. He is scarcely mentioned in Vincent's letters to others but seems to have been a negative presence for her, an emotional black hole.[8] She did not see him for eleven years. In contrast, her mother, Cora, also so frequently absent physically, provided a meaningful psychic presence for her daughter. Cora was herself a creative, intelligent, musical person (she played instruments at dances and the organ at church) and was wont to write songs, stories, and poems (occasionally published in small magazines). She was interested in theatricals and had the quality of making work into play for the children. All three of her daughters were beautiful and talented. Her second daughter, Norma, when an old lady, described Cora to Milford (2001) as a kind of impresario: "She was not

---

[8] Epstein (2001) states that there are no letters from Henry Millay in the retained family letters before 1912, when Edna went to visit him on what was supposed to be his deathbed.

like anyone else's mother. She made us—well, into her per-
formers" (9). There is a sense in which being mother's perfor-
mers continued for all three daughters. Edmund Wilson gives
an impression of Cora, whom he first met when she was an old
woman: "All three [daughters] were [talented] and extremely
pretty. But it was the mother who was most extraordinary. . . .
She had anticipated the Bohemianism of her daughters; and
she sometimes made remarks that were startling from the lips
of a little old lady. But there was nothing sordid about her; you
felt even more than with Edna that she had passed beyond
good and evil, beyond the power of hardship to worry her, and
that she had attained there a certain gaiety" (1952, 760).

Vincent, as the oldest and probably the brightest, seems
to have been both more overindulged than her younger sisters
and yet used perforce as *the* responsible substitute household
caretaker by her mother. Edna organized their housekeeping
efforts in a playful and inspired way derived from her mother.
Cora Millay, in spite of often having been unavailable when
needed, could, when she was there, bully them and worry over
them, alternating between encouraging their artistic interests
(she taught Edna to read at five by reading her poetry), playing
with them, and letting them do as they pleased.[9]

In her teens, Millay was much given to daydreams and
extended fantasies, many of which she wrote down. She was a
dedicated diarist. At sixteen, Edna started a diary while her
mother was away. She called her diary "Ole Mammy Hush-
Chile," addressing it in her entries as if it were a person. She
writes Mammy that it was a comfort to confide in someone
who was "so nice and cuddly and story-telly when you're all

[9] Edna was taught music by her mother soon after. Milford quotes her
as saying, "I loved music more than anything in the world except my mother"
(2001, 25).

full of troubles and worries and little vexations" (Milford 2001, 29). Writing in the diary meant identifying with her mother and also providing a fantasy substitute for her presence.

Being "Spoiled" and Its Results

During those early years after the father was banished and the mother and girls were so dependent on relatives, Cora insisted that her daughters behave modestly and properly in the presence of others. They generally obeyed. Wildness and disobedience were suppressed, but, as evidenced by her documented subsequent behavior, Edna came through her childhood not sufficiently able to say no to her own perfervid impulses. In this she mirrored and, again, identified with her spirited, willful mother.

In 1908, at sixteen, Millay wrote a poem to her mother that shows her intense positive feelings toward her. The poem deals explicitly with undoing future separation from her; but the ongoing *threat* of loss is implicit:

> Dearest, when you go away
>   My heart will go too
> Will be with you all the day,
>   All the night with you.
> Where you are through lonely years,
>   There my heart will be.
> I will guide you past all fears
> And bring you back to me. (quoted in Milford
>   2001, 41)

Milford points out that the young poet is to be the one who protects her mother. The maternal role of controlling and protecting the precious dependent other, so much a part of

her childhood and youth in relation to her sisters; was sometimes lived out by Millay as an adult. She could be generous to
the needy and persecuted, especially in relation to causes and
strangers; for example, she gave money and time and raised
money and wrote and published about victims like Sacco and
Vanzetti and those massacred by the Nazis in Lidice. In her
narcissism, she usually avoided dependency by putting herself
first. Less often she sought out dependency by accepting care
from others—transiently from lovers whom she abandoned and
eventually and more lastingly from her indulgent husband.

Millay's Impatience, Envy, and Rage

As she grew older, and especially after she left home, Millay
was burdened by her need for instant gratification. This urgent
impatience probably stemmed from the torment of childhood
experience of years of being kept waiting.[10] The child spent almost every day and sometimes weeks waiting for Cora to come
home from her nursing duties, and she also suffered the chronic,
vain longing for her father to fulfill his tantalizing promises to
visit her. The passive dependency on needed others who were
not there for her as a child was, as she grew up, reversed to a
compulsion to control others. This compulsion, fueled by the
success evoked by her beauty and talent, allowed Millay to
frustrate and torment the many people who fell in love with
her; she could keep them waiting and longing for *her*.

Envy Begets Rage

Edna, who had the burdensome but perhaps also soul-
nourishing role of chief parental caretaker for her two younger

---

[10] Robert Fliess (1956, 107) illustrated impatience as "the cannibalistic
affect" in relation to the impatience of Shylock, hungry for flesh.

sisters, was still thereby subject to an enhancement of the sibling envy that had begun with their births. She also had to deal
with envy of her father's new wife and family, and the more ir-
rational envy of the patients on whom Cora lavished her gift
for caring, at the expense of neglecting her children. Vincent's
envy must have threatened to become more intense as she grew
into her teens, and the resultant rage and depression (rage
turned inward) must have been hard to bear. (Norma Millay,
after Edna's death, talked about her sister's "sudden rages," and
Cora wrote about her daughter's having sometimes become
wild as a child [see Milford, 33].) Vincent (age sixteen) wrote
in her diary, "I know I am going to explode. I know just how a
volcano feels before an eruption" (see Milford, 35). The hatred
and depression probably reached a climax in the year or so before Millay left home at twenty, when her mother worked out
of town for long periods. Edna herself was often physically ill,
and her sisters alternatively clung dependently on and were
provocative and ungrateful toward their older sibling. Edna, at
nineteen, exhausted by sickness and her household duties, was
trying to work on her long poem "Renascence," the publication of which would make her famous. The poem expresses
hope for rebirth after death. God, who provides the spiritual
renaissance in the poem, would have been a literary projection
of the teenager's much-needed rescuing parent. Millay was, after
the publication of "Renascence," never more than playfully religious, and references to God in her later poems are little more
than poetic lip service. Despite the intermittently suppressed
envy, rage, sadness, and frustration, her adolescence was also
full of times predominated by fun and creativity.

And the adult poet remembered her childhood, even after
her father's departure, as having been very happy. In a letter
written in 1948 (she was then fifty-seven, and bad memories
may have faded) in reply to a friend who had sent her pictures

of houses she and her mother and sisters had lived in when she
was a girl in Camden, Millay writes, "If my childhood and girl-
hood had not been so extraordinarily happy, I could not, of
course, study with such pure delight every aspect of these pic-
tured houses."

The letter goes on to spell out some of the closeness to,
and more than a bit of the identification with, her inventive and
artistically creative mother. Mutual interest is explicitly expressed
in what follows in this letter in relation to their shared passionate lifelong love of (again!) spring, gardens, and flowers:

> I remember the nasturtiums, climbing ones, which
> grew every year over the trellis of the porch at 80
> Washington Street—higher than the roof of the
> porch they always grew, and *Mother* was proud of
> this, and would make everybody who came there
> look at them and admit that this was so. She loved
> nasturtiums, the smell of the blossoms, and the
> velvety feel of them, and the rich colors. (And I do,
> too, *and I still can't abide the double ones!*)[11] For no
> matter how busy she was—and I suppose she was
> about as busy every minute of the time as it is pos-
> sible for a person to be—she always planted them
> herself; and yet, the planting of nasturtium seeds is
> a thing that could well be trusted to any fairly intel-
> ligent child: they sprout easily and grow well, no
> matter how you plant them; *they are not poisonous*

[11] What is the meaning of this cryptic statement? Perhaps the love for
"Mother" would acquire ambiguity if and when it grew too intense. The
flower's name means, etymologically, "nose twister"; this emphasizes the
sense of smell and may have evoked not only the smelling of flowers but the
inhaling of cocaine. Drug dealers of both sexes in fiction and life are sometimes called Mother by their addict clients.

> to eat *(though they are rather hot on the tongue, as*
> *I remember it,—anyway, we used to put them in*
> *pickles);* they sprout easily and grow well. (1952,
> 350–51; emphasis added)

How much was poison and how much was nutriment is not clear. There may be an unconscious link to her morphine and alcohol addictions in the poet's words here. (That nasturtiums are edible and labeled as "not poisonous"[12] in the rhapsodic memory by the poet in the 1948 letter seems fraught with conflicting feelings about "Mother.")

Mother's Death

Millay's mother died in February 1931 (the poet was then almost forty). Two months later she wrote to friends, after a trip with her husband to visit them in New York City: "Darlings, I knew that you were sorry. But there's nothing to say. We had a grand time. But it's a changed world. The presence of that absence is everywhere" (1952, 244).

A poem written after Cora Millay's death contains a "there is no life without mother" message, full of ambiguity:

> In this mound, and what's beneath,
> Is my cure, if cure there be;
> *I must starve or eat your death*
> *Till it nourish me.* (1931; emphasis added)[13]

---

[12] This is possibly another *negation*—covering an unconscious conviction that the flowers *were* poisonous.

[13] Cheney (1975) cites one of Millay's poems, "Prayer to Persephone," in which Persephone is queen of Hell. In it the poet "implores Persephone to take a maternal, protective role to comfort" (25) a beloved young friend from Vassar (Dorothy Colton) who died in the influenza epidemic of 1918. The goddess would supply flowers for the dead child.

Letters to Mother

Some of the happy and playful feelings about exchange of gifts
of flowers, trees, and plants is expressed in a letter Edna sent to
Cora a year before her mother's death: "One of the little white
lilacs that you dragged out of the ground by the hair of the
head and we planted by the sunken garden IS IN BLOSSOM!
I enclose a scrap of it. It is the first one to bloom. Next year
maybe they all will blossom! Isn't that thrilling? Also, your pine
is doing very well [and] every one of the cunning little yellow
tulips that you carried around in your handbag . . . under an
apple tree, every one of them blossomed this spring. [We]
thank you for them" (1952, 236–37).

Edna's letters to Cora are full of pet names, "darlings,"
and a variety of endearments. Yet here is an excerpt from a
letter of Edna's from 1927 that conveys something of the pressure Cora Millay could put onto her daughters. Youngest sister
Kathleen was about to publish her first book of poems:

> Dearest Mumbles:
>   I wrote Kathleen ages ago about her book. I told
> you I would, & I did and that's that. Now will you
> please stop worrying? Kathleen is about to publish
> a book, as thousands have done before her. A per-
> son who publishes a book willfully appears before
> the populace with his pants down. And there's noth-
> ing you can do about that. Kathleen is not a baby.
> And she has been struggling for years to be allowed
> to manage her own affairs. If she knew the kind of
> letter you wrote me on her behalf, she'd froth at the
> mouth & spit brimstone. . . . All your stewing and
> fretting will accomplish just one end: it will make

you very sick, & a nuisance to yourself, and a care to
everybody. . . . Won't you just R E L A X? (1952, 220)

Milford (2001) quotes an undated and unpublished poem
by Millay about her mother and her sisters that seems chiefly
addressed directly to Cora. It is titled, "Thoughts of Any Poet
at a Family Reunion":

> Would I achieve my stature,
> I must eschew *the you* within my nature,
> The loving notes that cry
> "*Our* mother!" and the "*I, I, I*"
> Name you, claim you, tame you *beyond doubt my*
> *creature!*
> Cool on a migrant wing, if I sing at all,
> Down-gliding, up-carried,
> Free must be over mountain and sea my call,
> Unsistered, unmarried (10; emphasis added)

And the biographer wisely adds, "Unsistered, unmarried. But
what she did not say—what she never said—was unmoth-
ered" (10). The poem also left out but could have included
"unfathered."

Henry Millay

There was a crucial turning point to sexual action and toward
separation from Cora when, in 1917, Edna (she was then twenty)
visited her sick father, who was expected to die very soon. She
had had ambivalent but probably primarily hostile feelings toward the father, who she felt had abandoned her as a child.[14]

---

[14]This was somewhat unfair; Edna was probably aware that her
mother had forced him to leave.

Cora was away nursing, and it was decided that Edna would go
to Kingman (near Bangor) to say goodbye to him as he lay on
what was expected to be his deathbed. It was a momentous
visit for both of them. Henry Millay was very glad to be with
his beautiful firstborn daughter, whom he had not seen for so
many years, and observers attributed his will to live and his recovery in large part to his joy at her presence. She saw him
daily, read to him, joked with him, and found him charming
and lovable. The pleasant encounter with her father seems to
me to have marked a turning point in her life. She had, during
the previous two years when her mother was working away
from their home village so much of the time, taken over completely the management of the household. Working hard at
cleaning and housekeeping—but especially at being the substitute mother in charge of her provocative, demanding, fond
but intermittently ungrateful younger sisters—took all her in-
genuity and proved a great physical as well as emotional strain;
she lost weight and became ill. At nineteen she felt condemned
to a kind of domestic slavery that interfered with her poetry
writing. [15] Leaving home and being in Bangor, where she felt so
welcome and cared for, made for relief. She uncharacteristically avoided writing to her mother (who expected daily reports), and, despite her mother's reproachful letters ordering
her to come home to Camden, Edna prolonged her visit for

---

[15] Some of Edna's suppressed hostility toward her mother for making
her do domestic service became evident after her marriage in her hostility
and even cruelty to her own servants, whose ill-use by her was a continual
problem. Only the repeated apologetic interventions of Edna's long-suffering
husband kept some of them from quitting. Millay would write tirades about
servants in her letters (see Epstein 2001, 195). Servants and waiters are often
unconscious scapegoats for parental imagoes.

several more delightful weeks—full of dances, visits, and a love affair. She was living in the house of her father's doctor. There she shared a bed with his daughter, Ella, four years older than Edna. Ella fell in love with Vincent and easily seduced the younger woman to lesbian sexuality.[16] But both of the young women, especially Millay, also flirted with the local men who flocked around the pretty newcomer.

"Renascence" and Vassar

After this rebellious taste of independence and sexual activity she returned to her mother's house. Within a month (April 1912) she started to work again on, and soon completed, her long poem "Renascence."[17] Its publication brought national recognition and led to the penniless girl's being sponsored and financed by a rich patroness/alumna to attend college at Vassar. There she was idealized, adored for her beauty and her artistic gifts.

Addiction as Related to Her Parents

As an adult, the beautiful and admired Edna became bisexually promiscuous (not uncommon in the artistic and literary Greenwich Village crowd in the 1920s), fond of gambling, and addicted to alcohol and, after an injury in a car accident, to morphine.[18] (Cora Millay was apparently unconcerned about

---

[16] After Edna left, Ella wrote to her praising her genitals (see Epstein 2001, 56).

[17] According to Epstein (2001), Millay always celebrated April as her turning point toward fame.

[18] "My candle burns at both ends;/It will not last the night;/ But oh my foes and oh my friends—/It casts a lovely light" (Millay 1920, 127).

the promiscuity of her daughters, saying that they were just doing what she had done at their age.)

Edna's reunion as a teenager with her father seemed to have launched a career of bisexuality. At college, there were homosexual contacts with other students (not unusual at Vassar in those days) in which Edna played the role of the one in control—teasing, jilting, and abandoning girl after girl. She was defiant and provocative toward college rules and authorities, but she was always eventually treated as an entitled exception owing to her forceful, charming personality, her talents as an actress in the school plays, and what was regarded as her genius as a poet.

Gradually her predominant sexual activity centered on men, unmarried and married. This sexual drive became more compulsively enacted after college. When she moved to New York City with her sister Norma, she had one affair after another, often more than one at the same time. She received many marriage proposals but didn't take them seriously. Leaving in order not to be left was her specialty. Cruelty was interspersed with real concern and caring, as it had been with the Vassar girls.

Millay could also, particularly outside the realm of passionate love and sex, be both thoughtful and generous to her friends. Her magnanimity and openhandedness were often forthcoming when lovers or former lovers were in emotional and financial troubles not connected with her neglect and rejection of them. Men and women (her homosexual interest seemed to lessen after college) were drawn to her because of her beauty, wit, and seductiveness. She had longer affairs with many talented men, including the great critic-to-be Edmund Wilson, the novelist Floyd Dell, and the poet Witter Bynner. She stated that she felt she could love two men at the same time (see Cheney

1975, 92). Wilson was one of the few "strong" male lovers with whom friendship continued after an affair had ended.

Weak and dependent men almost always evoked her sadism. She seems to have taken an especial pleasure in breaking up marriages, probably unconsciously taking revenge on her parents. Leaving others, to illustrate the theme of this book, meant identifying with the parents of her childhood. Guilt and remorse in the form of needing punishment and illness frequently followed her misbehavior and acts of rejection. She tended to maintain a continuing attraction to men who kept their distance from or left *her* (as her father had). An example was her long relationship with another strong man, Arthur Ficke, a fellow-poet and a married man who for a long time warded off Edna's attempt to seduce him. He finally succumbed but subsequently kept away from her bed yet continued as a loyal friend (although their affair may have occasionally resumed for awhile once they were both married to others).

Edna was a sort of bisexual Don Giovanni, flitting from conquest to conquest, with touches of Mozart's hero's sadism and provocative defiance.[19] Sometimes there were two or three sexual partners on the same day. Her initial desire and commitment to a man could quickly lead to indifference and then separation—leaving them as her parents had left her. She always had to be the one in control of the relationship. Yet when her dominance was resisted, there was a great urgency to undo the other's power or indifference and a need to pursue the relationship. In these sexual affairs, there was a revival of her sado-masochistic attachment to her parents, but now as active rejecter and abandoner, able to haunt her ex-lovers.

[19] The apt title of Nancy Milford's biography of Millay is *Savage Beauty* (2001).

Bisexual Men

Millay had a particular interest in sleeping with bisexual but predominantly homosexual men (and in a ménage à trois including them).[20] Perhaps they were unconsciously idealized to represent what she wanted to be: both male and female, with fantasies of having and becoming both—and also of being mother and father as well as child. She seems to have wanted to be desirable enough to convert men who loved men to loving *her*. (Her enacted bisexuality was manifested in occasional transient lesbian contacts even after her sexual compulsion centered chiefly on men.)

Several writer/ex-lovers have expressed the opinion that every man she met not only wanted to take her to bed but to marry her; some of these men were homosexual (for example, Witter Bynner). But Edna had no intention of marrying anyone in those Greenwich Village years of her early twenties. She had a Proustian tendency (like her mother before her) to try to set up some sort of ménage à trois with two men that, unlike that of Leonard Woolf and the Parsons (see next chapter), never could have worked out.[21]

Weak lovers were quickly and usually permanently discarded. The strong, in character and talent, were also eventually dismissed as lovers. Millay appears to have been more deeply attached—here in a masochistic way—to those few who became,

[20] Cheney (1975) writes that among her more than casual lovers there were three men of literature who were predominantly homosexual: Witter Bynner, Alan Ross Macdougal, and Harrison Dowd (115).

[21] Epstein describes an occasion of another kind of ménage à trois when Edna, Edmund Wilson, and his friend John Peale Bishop shared a bed in some sort of "top and bottom" threesome arrangement: that adds erogenic to the bisexual connotations of her "My candle burns at both ends" poem.

or remained, sexually indifferent to her (these were mostly older men) or who threatened to leave or left her for other women.

Being and Having Father

Conflicts about belonging to, being like, and reacting to (submitting to and resisting) her mother dominated Edna St. Vincent Millay's life, for better and for worse. But similar (although weaker) ties to her father are also apparent in her frequent affairs, which could begin with great promise but usually ended badly. There was an aura of incest about the few lovers (all male) with whom she formed longer attachments. There were at least three significant long-term ones in which two men were old enough to be father figures,[22] and one, George Dillon, a twenty-one-year-old poet she met when she was thirty-six, became a kind of son.

Later Life

Millay's later life was modified by a predominantly successful marriage at thirty-two to a man twelve years her elder, Eugen Boissevain, who protectively indulged her and took over what are usually a wife's responsibilities in relation to home and meals. He had previously been married to a remarkable woman to whom he was extremely devoted.[23] She had died early in their marriage, six years before he met Millay. He had a self-sacrificing, sometimes masochistic, yet benevolent and even heroic per-

[22] E.g., Arthur Ficke.

[23] This was Inez Milholland, a well-known suffragette. She had visited and lectured at Vassar when Millay was a student there. Inez had led the Suffragette Parade riding a white horse down Fifth Avenue in New York City. Edna wrote that Milholland was "the idol of the undergraduates" (1952, 316) at Vassar. After her marriage to Boissevain, Millay dedicated a sonnet to Milholland.

sonality,[24] acting toward Edna as a dedicated nurse who both indulged and helped her control her addictions and nursed her through her "small nervous breakdowns" (see Cheney 1975, 73, 91).[25] Boissevain was a mother with a penis who was able to fulfill wishes and satisfy or tolerate whims.

Boissevain was wealthy and could and wanted to give his beautiful genius wife whatever she wanted. He was able to be self-effacing enough to say, "It is so obvious to anyone that Vincent is more important than I am" (quoted by Cheney 1975, 122). Later on his income decreased, and she earned enough from her royalties and lecture fees to become their chief financial provider. Boissevain brought a comparative calm and stability to her way of living. In 1925, the couple bought and renovated an old farmhouse in Austerlitz, New York; the place was a safe home base for Edna. Boissevain managed the external details of her daily routines, drawing her bath, rubbing her back (as mother Cora had done when Millay was a child). He was able to accept her needs for drugs and for lovers (and even for occasional long excursions with them outside New York and to Europe).[26] He was always there to supply benevolent parental care so that she could write, lecture, and live like a willful child when she wished or needed to. When he died sud-

[24] He once jumped into the treacherous Seine river during a storm to save a drowning would-be suicidal Parisian woman. Cheney describes Boissevain as "a skilled athlete" (1975, 112).

[25] The quote is from Edmund Wilson in relation to events of the early 1920s. Wilson was a kind of predecessor of Boissevain as a nursing parent in Edna's early village days; he often looked after her when she was drunk and arranged for and took care of her after an abortion. There were more frequent minor "nervous breakdowns" during the last twenty years of Millay's life. Their nature is not clear; they could have been partly hysterical. Wilson wrote, "There was something of awful drama about everything one did with Edna" (1952, 752).

[26] For example, going to Paris with her young lover, George Dillon. Boissevain also had extramarital affairs, with Edna's knowledge.

denly of an unsuspected cancer in 1949, she outlived him for only a little over a year. It is hard not to assume she couldn't survive without the promise of his care. And with his death, there was to be no life for her without mother. (Edmund Wilson [1952, 784] wrote that he once heard Boissevain call Edna "my child.")[27]

After her marriage her lovers were mostly younger men, and usually the affairs were carried on intermittently and only with one man at a time. She remained addicted to morphine (her habit supported by permissive physicians) for a good part of her later adult life.[28] Her work was both popular and lucrative during most of her lifetime, but her role as a major poet, a widely held judgment during her first two decades as a published writer, has subsequently been challenged by many. Millay's life currently attracts more popular interest than her poetry. Her work is lyric rather than intellectual, and her style has been regarded as old-fashioned—more nineteenth century than twentieth—but she was intelligent, possessed critical acumen, and, especially in her earlier work, produced very beautiful and moving poems. After her mother's death, Millay's poetic creativity continued, but the quality of her poems seemed diminished. Still, Wilson, a great if biased critic, felt that Mil-

---

[27] In 1949, just before Edna's husband's death, Edmund Wilson visited the couple at Steepletop. Wilson had not seen her in nineteen years, and she had visibly aged and seemed frightened, her hands shaking. He writes, "[Eugen] very quietly watched her and managed her. At moments he would baby her in a way I had not seen him use before but that had evidently become habitual, when she showed signs of bursting into tears over not being able to find a poem or something of the kind" (1932, 784).

[28] From a 1935 letter to her former lover and friend Witter Bynner: "I am at present under the influence of hashish, gin, bad poetry, love, morphine and hunger. Otherwise I could not be writing you even this" (quoted by Cheney 1975, 124.) By that time Millay needed drugs even for the effort of being a hostess at the Boissevain home, Steepletop.

lay was one of the few contemporary American poets whose work approached the greatness of the major nineteenth- and twentieth-century authors of poetry in English.

Good-and-Bad Haunting

The "renascence" at twenty of a relationship with her father had launched a course of defiant sexual and general independence— but not from the parents (good and bad versions of both mother and father) lurking within her unconscious mind.

Millay's life provides an instance of how much independence, authenticity, accomplishment, and creativity can exist alongside the pathology that accompanies the continuing or revived attachment to the internalized early parent I have been discussing. It is to be noted that, for the poet, her parents—especially her mother, both as example and as source of identification— evoked and induced both psychic health (creativity) and psychic pathology. Wilson, in his discerning and balanced assessment and tribute to the woman he had once loved and wanted to marry, points out the pressure of nervous strain even in her early Greenwich Village years—and he calls the last part of Millay's life the period of her as "the neurotic invalid" (1952, 752). But he also pays high tribute to her capacity for emotional health in her personal and creative life, writing of "the formidable strength of character that lay behind her attractiveness and brilliance" (757).[29] It was a strength she shared with and derived from her mother.

Edna's was largely a mother-haunted existence; there are good and bad witches, and parental haunting has good, bad, and good-and-bad consequences.

---

[29] Wilson writes that Edna's "power of enhancing and ennobling life was felt by all who knew her" (1952, 745).

tombstone were inscribed the words of the prophet Micah that he had once told Leonard: "What doth the Lord require of thee, but to do justly, and to love mercy, and to walk humbly with thy God?" (Woolf 1960, 15).

Woolf (1960) writes in *Sowing* that he always felt he was his mother's least favorite child.[1] He describes his mother, Marie Woolf, as she was in the years after his father's death with a cool, objective bitterness:

> What made her a curious character was the strange mixture in her psychology of toughness and softness. To hear her talk you would sometimes have concluded that she was living in a world of complete unreality. And so up to a point she did. She lived in a dream world which centered in herself and her nine children. It was the best of all possible worlds, a fairyland of nine perfect children worshipping a mother to whom they owed everything, loving one another, and revering the memory of their deceased father. Nothing that actually happened, no fact, however *black*,[2] however inconsistent with the dream, made her doubt its reality and its *rosiness*.[3] . . . She loved all her nine surviving

[1] The first of his five volumes of autobiography was mostly written and all were published when he was an old man in his eighties.

[2] Blackness recurs in the material I am going to quote from Woolf's writings. Freud is said to have remarked that the black man is the father in the dark. Both Woolf's dead father and the father from his primal scene fantasies as a child could in this sense be evoked by this color. So could his mother in her mourning dress.

[3] Rosiness is mother's color, as black is father's. Did this condition Woolf's love of roses and flowers? The red and the black may have been Woolf's colors of the primal scene. On the other hand, long after his father's death, Marie Woolf still was the widow dressed in black.

children, *but she loved me less, I think, than any of
the eight others,* because she felt me to be unsympathetic to her view of the family, of the universe and
of the relation of one to the other. (1960, 21; emphasis added)

Blackness existed for him alongside the rosiness of her fairy-
land, and the stress on his being his father's child resulted in
the need to enact *not* being his mother's for most of his life—
at least in his conscious mind. He also was able to report that
in contrast to her existence in the "dream world of *rosy* sentimentality and unreality, she was at the same time an extremely
practical, sensible, hard-headed woman" (22; emphasis added).
She showed determination and courage in dealing with the practical difficulties of raising her children with insufficient funds.

Woolf's mother lived to be ninety-one, dying in 1939,
several years before Virginia's suicide. Leonard was fifty-nine
when Marie Woolf died. Spater and Parsons quote from a letter
of Virginia Woolf's in which she wrote, obviously not fondly,
that in her old age, her mother-in-law was "as spry as a weasel"
(1977, xiv).[4] When Marie Woolf died, Leonard (1901–69) wrote
in a letter, "[Mother] died earlier in the year. She was 88 [*sic*], but
in mind and body invincible. . . . She fell against a table in her
room and broke a rib and the shock was too much for her" (245).

Weltschmertz in the Gardens of Childhood

Leonard, as the third oldest and least favorite of the children,
must have experienced the new baby's arrival every year with

[4]When Leonard and Virginia married, they (in mutual agreement)
did not invite Leonard's mother or any of his family to the wedding.

little cast of "rosiness." Leonard's next sibling was born when he was two, and they kept arriving almost every year thereafter, six more between 1882 and 1889 (when Leonard was nine). It is most probable that another one was anticipated during the family's summer vacation when he was five. Of this momentous summer, he writes, "Every year in the last week of July or the first of August the whole Woolf family went away for a summer holiday in the country" (27). The cosmic depressive reaction ("my first experience of *Weltschmerz*") took place in *an enclosed space,* a dirty enclosed space, the family garden, on the return from this vacation: "Behind [our] house was a long parallelogram *enclosed by the house on the north and on the other three sides* by three *grimy* six-foot walls. It was a typical London garden of that era, consisting of a worn parallelogram of grass surrounded by narrow gravel paths and then narrow beds of *sooty, sour London soil* against the walls. Each child was given a few feet of bed for his own personal 'garden' and there we sowed seeds. . . . It was here that I first experienced a wave of that profound, cosmic melancholia which is hidden in every human heart and can be heard at its best—or should one say worst?—in the infant crying *in the night* with no language but a cry" (26–27; emphasis added). On the family's return, the boy rushed out "eagerly to see the back garden," and what starts with great promise ends in disappointment, depression, and anxiety. The garden is now dirtier, barren, and infested:

> There it lay in its *grimy* solitude. There was not a breath of air. There were no flowers; a few spindly lilac bushes drooped in the beds. The *grimy* ivy drooped on the *grimy* walls. And all over the walls from ivy leaf to ivy leaf were large or small spiderwebs, dozens and dozens of them, quite motionless,

and motionless in the centre of each sat a large or a
small, a fat or a lean spider. I stood by myself in the
patch of scurfy grass and contemplated the spiders;
I can still smell the smell of sour earth and ivy; *and
suddenly* my whole mind and body seemed to be
overwhelmed in *melancholy*. I had experienced for
the first time, without understanding it, that sense
of cosmic unhappiness which comes upon us when
we *look* out of *darkened* windows, when the daughters of *music* are laid low, the doors are shut in the
street, the *sound* of the grinding is low, the grasshop-
per is a burden and desire fails. (27–28; my emphasis for connections with dirt and blackness, sight
and sound)

The quotation's last sentence, poetic but cryptic and confusing
(where was the copy editor?), seems to emphasize looking and
listening leading to the failure of desire. One wonders about
the symbolism of the spider, evoking the *vagina dentata* and
cannibalistic connotations (black widow?) in an (anal) setting
of blackness, dirt, and degradation. Terror and foreboding were
produced as concomitants of an unconscious primal scene fantasy evoked by looking at the enclosed garden that symbolized
the mother's genitals—the symbol here first idealized and then
cloacally and anally degraded as the spider-ridden dirty *back*
garden. The garden experience that started out full of reliance
on the future ends in fear and foulness.

Woolf writes of the second occasion, when he was about
eight, "on which I felt the burden of a hostile universe weigh
down upon my spirit" (28). It again involves a garden, another
of the family's yearly summer vacations, and perhaps also his
mother's last pregnancy during that year. He describes the

family arriving at a new house on a cliff above the sea: "After tea I wandered out by myself to explore the garden. The house and garden were quite new for the garden was almost bare. Along the side facing the sea ran a long low mound or rampart. I sat there in the sunshine looking down on the sparkling water. It smelt and felt so good after the long hours in the stuffy train. *And then suddenly* quite near me out of a hole in the bank came two large *black-and-yellow* newts.[5] They did not notice me and stretched themselves out to bask in the sun. They entranced me and I forgot everything, including time, as I sat there with those strange beautiful creatures surrounded by blue sky, sunshine and sparkling sea" (28; emphasis added). Here is another potential primal scene fantasy that begins full of beautiful promise. But it again ends badly—light is endangered by darkness and blackness: "I do not know how long I had sat there when, all at once, I felt afraid.[6] I looked up and saw that an enormous *black thunder cloud* had crept up and now covered more than half of the sky. It was just *blotting out the sun*, and, as it did so, the newts *scuttled back into their hole*. It was terrifying and, no doubt, I was terrified" (28–29; emphasis added). Woolf had used the word "cosmic" to describe his unhappiness. It also could be applied to his terror—terror of sex and of death. The changes here brought about by separation, maturation, and perhaps trauma portend, alongside excitement and promise, overwhelming loss—castration anxiety and loss of mother (symbolized by earth, home, garden) and father (symbolized by the sun). Woolf's feelings seem to me to express the terror of change that was expressed by my patient's question: "Is there life without mother?" As A. E. Hous-

---

[5] This is the second time that Woolf mentions *sudden* change—compare patient X's "And suddenly!" phenomena derived from Handel's *Messiah*.
[6] A third "and suddenly!"

man (1922) put it, "I, a stranger and afraid / In a world I never made" (poem XII). Spotts (1989) comments about the pessimism acquired in Woolf's childhood: "It was no doubt at this critical age that there took root the 'fatalistic and half-amused resignation' that he said was his deepest trait" (4).

Woolf was happy and successful as a student at Cambridge. He made lifelong friends and became a member of the exclusive band—they called themselves the Apostles—who gathered around the philosopher G. E. Moore. After graduation he did not know what he should do. He had to earn a living and decided the only way he could do it was to join the foreign service. He was assigned to Ceylon. Leaving England and his friends was a misery for him.

Ceylon

Leonard Woolf became successful and a forceful independent adult during his lonely and miserable years doing a variety of jobs of increasing responsibility in Ceylon. He was given his own district to manage after only a few years in Ceylon—an unusually short time for such a post. He writes in 1909 in a letter to Moore,

> You say you don't think you have changed at all. I think I have a good deal. This sort of work becomes an obsession; I do about 12 hours a day. The district of which I am in charge is about 1000 square miles & one is responsible for nearly everything in it. I mean in keeping order, collecting the revenue & doing innumerable other things with roads & irrigation works & education, besides acting as Police Magistrate & judge in civil cases. One has of course

to be continually travelling through the district & there is of course no railway & very often no roads. . . . It is almost always too hot & one rarely feels absolutely well, food is disgusting & there is very little water & what there is is brackish. Also there is no one to talk to at all. The nearest white man lives 20 miles away. (1901–69, 144)

But Woolf was able to do the job and do it well. According to Spotts (1989), Woolf in later life called his service there his second birth. Spotts writes, "He was highly competent, drove himself remorselessly and made himself so indispensable that wherever he served, he soon became the person who was really in charge. . . . And he proved he could do equally well with peasants, British planters, village headmen, whores, colonial governors, and retired empresses"[7] (57, 64).

He was able to handle a variety of emergencies, worked as a judge as well as an administrator, carried out many special assignments, including organizing famine relief, directing and bringing order to a busy pearl fishery,[8] and many other tasks.[9] He learned the local languages, was able to mix with and be respected by the natives—his interest in them as human beings was exceptional among the British administrators. He wrote a novel about Ceylon and the Ceylonese, *The Village in the Jungle,* (1913). It was written mostly in Ceylon in his scant spare time.

[7] Empress Eugenie visited Ceylon in 1908, and Leonard had to be her host when she visited his district.

[8] "There is a huge camp of 40,000 people. There are only 4 Europeans supervising the whole thing . . . there will be not time for anything but work. It is supposed to be very unhealthy, and everyone says I am a fool to go" (1901–69, 113).

[9] See Spotts 1989, 60, for a half-page-long list of Woolf's accomplishments in Ceylon.

The novel received warm critical attention in England, and his handling of the native characters is still praised as true to life and honored in Ceylon. When he returned to England for a year's leave in 1911, he felt he loved and missed Ceylon, and he would have returned if Virginia had refused to marry him. With the prospect of her saying yes, he resigned from the civil service and remained in England.

Personally, however, for much of the years he spent in Ceylon, especially the first four or five, he predominately hated what he was doing and the conditions of his life. He hated his separation from his friends, especially from Lytton Strachey, to whom he wrote most of his many letters during his years there. He couldn't stand the boredom, and he couldn't stand his colleagues, and he couldn't stand the dirt and the foulness and misery in the lives of the natives. "Foulness" is a word that recurs frequently in his letters. There are also many misogynous references to the British ladies, their dullness, snobbery, and their ugliness—which he often mentions. His feelings toward the whores he frequented were more positive, but he couldn't help also despising himself and from time to time also them for his sexual dependency on them. Dirt and blackness and foulness abound. He writes to Strachey, "It is only when I get your letters that I even think now. . . . To think of existence at all fills me with horror and sickness; the utter *foulness,* the stupid blind vindictive *foulness* of everything and of myself" (1901–69, 150; emphasis added). He several times considered suicide. He writes to Strachey in a letter of 1906, "I took out my gun the other night, made my will and prepared to shoot myself. God knows why I didn't. . . . I weep over the wreck and ruin of my existence" (1901–69, 118).

Yet Woolf was able to accomplish so much with his hard work, and he did it while retaining his decency and fairness toward the native people who were in his charge, despite his fundamental disapproval of the British colonial system—no Kipling, he. The terrible years and the considerable accomplishment made him more confident; he was now a man, not a Cambridge youth. He also had made himself into a writer, and when he returned from his seven years in Ceylon in 1911 he quickly began to publish essays and reviews in literary magazines. After his resignation, he soon married Virginia Stephen (as Strachey had been urging him to do intermittently for years in his letters).

Marriage

In the course of their long marriage (1912–41), Woolf became a kind and caretaking, verging on a maternal husband to Virginia Woolf—almost more of a companion and, in her recurrent attacks of mental illness, more of a nurse than a spouse.[10] Like Edna St. Vincent Millay's similarly protective and maternal husband, Eugen Boissevain, Leonard was able to tolerate his wife's bisexuality and her rare sexual affairs (exclusively with women in the case of Virginia Woolf). She married him after telling him that she cared about him but did not love him. A deep kind of devotion developed between them, but it did not include much sexual attraction to him on her part. There is some suggestion and much speculation that, after a wedding night in which Virginia was too afraid to allow intercourse, the two lived together platonically (or predominantly platonically). This was very hard for Leonard, but most of their friends felt that he was never unfaithful to Virginia out of fear that her finding it out would lead to another nervous breakdown. She

---

[10] Virginia's mother died when she was thirteen. Virginia wrote, "Her death was the greatest disaster that could happen" (quoted in Bell 1972, 42).

still broke down periodically—sometimes for periods of weeks to months from 1913 on and needed to be hospitalized in 1915 (three years after the marriage) after a suicide attempt. (She had taken an overdose of Veronal.) There followed twenty-five years of intermittent mental instability marked by repeated short breakdowns and near breakdowns, in between her sane and, especially in her writing, hard work and superior creative functioning. Leonard constantly looked after her and developed ways of getting her to rest and eat and of attenuating her obsessions and depressions during this time.[11] It was, for Virginia, despite the continual potential for danger, a time of predominantly happy companionship with Leonard, of great pleasure in busy social activity, of a long affair with her friend Victoria Sackville-West, and, above all, of great creativity as essayist and novelist. There is an essay on the Woolfs by Cynthia Ozick entitled "Mrs. Virginia Woolf: The Madwoman and the Nurse." Leonard is, of course, the nurse. He worried over her, tended to her, and encouraged and protected her.

The psychoanalyst Alix Strachey (wife of Lytton's psychoanalyst younger brother, James Strachey), who observed the situation firsthand over many years, expressed a view shared by almost everyone who knew and wrote about them (one feels all Bloomsbury wrote about them) when she said, "I am sure that [Leonard] was the only person who could have kept her going" (Spotts 1989, 160). Woolf was for his wife the kind of figure he would have wanted his mother to have been for him as a child.[12] The years of his childhood were spent in a

[11] The depressive disturbances seemed to come on especially just after she had published a book.

[12] Frederick Spotts, the editor of Leonard Woolf's *Letters (1901–1969)*, writes, "If there were a Nobel Prize for marriage, Leonard would deserve to be its laureate" (xi).

house full of servants. One wonders whether there had been a strong and perhaps warm attachment to a nursemaid or nanny that he turned to during his apparently unremembered and certainly undocumented earliest years. It could have been so, perhaps partly in needy reaction to having felt he was his mother's least favorite child. If there was such a mother-substitute, being Virginia's nurse would represent both a positive identification with the good mothering figure alongside a negative one with his own mother (= being NOT MOTHER, an unconscious, reproachful reaction)—thus simultaneously continuing in an active way both life *with* and *as* mother. The first is speculation; the Not Being Mother, a negative way to express being haunted by his mother, seems to me beyond doubt. Spotts (1989) implies, I feel, Leonard's masochistic role as the idealized mother, who cares so deeply that her "child" always comes first, when he observes, "From the first year of his marriage onward, then, Leonard's life was governed by Virginia's health. Whether to have children, where to live and the hours to keep, when to go out and when to have friends in, when to travel and when to stay home, all had to be decided with that in mind" (161).

Woolf's Sexual Life

Leonard, in an autobiographical story, "A Tale told by Moonlight" (from his "Stories from the East"), presents a commentary on imperialism based on his sexual and emotional experiences when frequenting native prostitutes during his seven years (1904–11) as a young man in Ceylon. He was then already in love with Virginia Stephen, the sister of another close Cambridge friend, Thoby Stephen. He had left England without declaring his love; he had little hope of the beautiful and intelli-

gent girl's being interested in him. In his peripatetic existence
while serving as a civil servant, ranging from sole administrator of various large Ceylonese districts to chief magistrate, he
had an active heterosexual life with prostitutes from and in native brothels. Leonard would write about these sexual exploits
in frequent letters to his prurient closest friend and (another)
fellow Cambridge graduate, Lytton Strachey,[13] a homosexual
who had himself been engaged, for one day before he changed
his mind, to Virginia Stephen.[14] Leonard had a most ambivalent attitude toward these native women. He was indignant with
the way the natives (and the Englishmen who ruled them) regarded and treated Ceylonese women, and, having learned to
speak both Talit and Sinhalese, he used to talk to and sympa-
thize with some of the women whom he paid for sex.[15] But
he also couldn't help despising them and thereby also himself—
alongside the empathy he felt. He was one of those men who
appears to have suffered to some degree (and at least for the
early part of his long adult life) from a split in sexual attitude,
sometimes called the madonna/whore complex. The designa-
tion applies to men who are able to be lustful and potent with
devalued women but are hesitant and frequently cannot function or enjoy sexual contact with (usually idealized) girlfriends
or wives, toward whom they may still feel great tenderness.

[13] Woolf, Strachey, and Thoby Stephens, Virginia's beloved brother,
were among the six Cambridge undergraduates who formed a literary club
called the Midnight Society. (Clive Bell, Vanessa Stephens's first husband,
was another of the six.)
[14] The two remained lifelong friends, and both talked freely about life
between "the buggers" of Cambridge, one of whom was Maynard Keynes.
Strachey was Leonard's best friend during his years in Ceylon. Woolf was
clearly not homosexual, as his sexual desires and actions involved women.
[15] The Tamils (minority) were Hindus and originally from India; the
Sinhalese (majority) were Moslems.

Woolf's active and compulsive sex in Ceylon brothels contrasts greatly with the, at least relatively, asexual life with Virginia.[16] Virginia Stephen felt threatened by male sexuality and perhaps by sexuality in general. She had been sexually abused as a young girl by both of her much older stepbrothers.[17]

Loss of Virginia

Virginia's death by suicide in 1941, after years of intermittent severe mental illness, was a terrible, an almost unendurable, loss for Leonard. Perhaps it gradually also became something of a relief and a liberation. But there can be no doubt that Leonard was for a very long time devastated by Virginia's suicide after so many years of marriage. Probably the terrible loss was made even worse in reaction to guilt induced by her suicide note, in which she had written that she was drowning herself in order not to go on spoiling his life (see Adamson 2001, xvi). Adamson quotes from a note Leonard wrote after Virginia's death that Trekkie Parsons (the much-beloved companion of his later, post-Virginia years) found among Leonard's papers after he died: "They say: 'Come to tea and let us comfort you.' But it's no good. One must be crucified on one's own private cross. It is a strange fact that *a terrible pain in the heart* can be interrupted by a little pain in the fourth *toe* of the right foot. I know that V. will not come across the garden from the lodge,

---

[16] There is dispute about this by biographers, and no conclusive data emerge from the writings of either Leonard or Virginia, but most of them and their contemporaries have the impression of sexual coolness on Virginia's part and a resigned, tolerant attitude toward this by Leonard. He certainly tolerated her homosexual affairs, which may still have caused him "a pain in the heart" (see letter that follows).

[17] Virginia never revealed the details of just what happened to her, beyond her being groped.

and yet I look in that direction for her. I know that she is
drowned, and yet I listen for her to come in at the door. I know
that it is the last page, and yet I turn it over. There is no limit
to one's stupidity and selfishness" (vxi; emphasis added; we
will hear more about toes).

Trekkie

After Virginia's death, change was not exclusively loss for him.
He did go on to have a close and, as gathered from his letters, a
predominantly happy intimate relationship (whatever its physical nature) during his last twenty-six or -seven years with Trekkie
Parsons, a much younger woman, an illustrator of books, and
a would-be painter. They met several months after Viginia's
death in 1941 (when their letters begin). They met occasionally
afterward but did not become really close until she wrote him
in the fall of 1942. She told Leonard in her letter that her husband was again being sent overseas by the military authorities
and asked if she could stay overnight with him at Monks House,
his country house. That night turned out to be the beginning
of a long period of Leonard and Trekkie's intermittently living
together at Monks House. By the end of 1943, the two were
deeply in love.

Trekkie was the wife of a friend, Ian Parsons, who worked
in publishing, as did Leonard.[18] Ian had been in France before
the affair started, serving as a staff officer in the RAF in World

---

[18] Ian worked for Chatto and Windus. The firm in the late 1930s
bought a half-share in Leonard's Hogarth Press; after this Leonard worked
with Parsons directly but lost some of his autonomy. Woolf continued to be
in charge of editing and publishing the English translations of Freud until
the whole set of *The Complete Psychological Works of Sigmund Freud* was
completed in 1966. (Woolf started publishing Freud translations in 1924.)

War II. Even when he returned to England from France, he would frequently be sent abroad on various missions for prolonged periods. On one of these long assignments, Trekkie stayed in Leonard's house for over a year. Ian was very much aware of the arrangement.

After Ian's discharge from the service, Woolf lived near the Parsons in the country, and they all three shared Woolf's quarters in London. Leonard, over the next twenty-odd years, often traveled and vacationed with Trekkie, leaving Ian (apparently not too unhappily) behind. Trekkie would also go on alternate vacations with Ian (to France, Switzerland, Italy, Austria, and America) and then with Leonard (to France, where he sometimes arrived as Ian was leaving, to Greece and Israel, and to Ceylon). She was apparently able to care about and care for both men, cooking their meals and tending to their quarters. Although hers was an independent spirit, Trekkie took almost maternal care of Leonard. It was deeply meaningful to Trekkie that Leonard believed in the importance of her gifts as an artist and painter—gifts she was masochistic enough to doubt and deprecate frequently. Trekkie and Leonard shared many interests, especially an impassioned fascination with gardens. Adamson (2001) calls both Trekkie and Leonard "first-rate gardeners" (44).[19]

Woolf wrote, "When at last the war ended and Ian was demobilized, a new rhythm of life began for us. I stayed one or two nights a week in [London] to do my work at The Hogarth Press and [at] various political committees; Trekkie did the same, but stayed with me at Rodmell in the middle of the week. We *cultivated our gardens passionately,* the Parsons at Iford

---

[19] In later years, Woolf had a yearly day on which the public could view his garden; proceeds went to charity.

and I at Rodmell" (nearby) (1969, 180; emphasis added).[20] The middle-aged widower had apparently found a younger caretaking (parental) companion. With Ian, they formed a very strange triangle, which seemed to work well for the most part for all three. For over twenty-five years, Trekkie Parsons, in happily spending part of the week with Woolf and part of the week with her lawful spouse, had in effect two husbands—openly in some ways, secretly in others. Was it only their gardens that Leonard and Trekkie cultivated passionately? It is not clear if Trekkie and Leonard were lovers, but from their letters (see Adamson 2001) they were clearly both deeply in love. In his *Autobiography,* Woolf writes of the Parsons as his "intimate friends" (1969, 112). Some writers are convinced that the affair was sexual (see Coates 1998, whose insistence that the two had a sexual relationship even when Virginia was alive seems to me based not on evidence but on her clear bias against Leonard Woolf.[21] Yet her view about the sex afterward might still be right.) Without more documentation, no one can be sure. Ian appears to have been something of a womanizer who, during the triangle years, certainly had at least one long-term sexual affair and some casual ones—complicating the ménage à trois but also making it more acceptable. (Adamson (2001) calls this "most unusual domestic compact" (xviii) a "*ménage à trois à trois ménages*" (*xxi).*[22] Ian and Leonard seem to have gotten along well and were able to work together at Hogarth Press after the war.

[20] Woolf was a dedicated gardener for most of his life, despite (or perhaps because of) his childhood traumatic garden experiences.

[21] Coates (1998) suggests that Leonard was "the facilitator and perhaps the reason for" Virginia's suicide. She believes in his unfaithfulness during his marriage (of which there is no definite evidence) as part of her determined attempt to depict Leonard Woolf as an exemplar of what an evil man can do to women.

[22] "A household of three affecting three households."

As Trekkie approached middle age, she began to suffer mild chronic menopausal depression, which made her unhappy—especially so in regard to her painting. She sometimes expressed dissatisfaction with her relationships with both men, but more with Ian than with Leonard. Leonard continued to be rapturous in his writing to her of his idealized love. Trekkie found herself resenting Ian's infidelities, especially his long-term relationship with a female colleague from Chatto and Windus. She continued to share Ian's social life and holidays abroad; they were generally much admired as a couple who danced together beautifully. But she wrote to Leonard on one of the vacations with Ian in 1957, "Being a wife, I never wanted to be a wife from as far as I can remember. I suppose because of this I dreamed last night that I threw a green exercise book at Ian here in a public meeting, and woke feeling we had had a quarrel which we hadn't" (Adamson 2001, 228).

Trekkie in her nineties denied that there had been sex between herself and Leonard. But then, long after Leonard had died, she may have wanted to protect his reputation as the devoted husband of Virginia Woolf (see Adamson 2001, xxiii). Adamson writes that Trekkie also probably felt that she didn't want to be "dismissed as Leonard's mistress" (xxiii). Most who have written about Leonard and Virginia do not doubt his continuing devotion to his dead wife, nor could anyone reading their letters to one another doubt his subsequent love for Trekkie or hers for him.[23] In his letters, he frequently wrote to her as "my dearest," and in hers he was usually "my darling Leonard."

[23] Virginia, understandably, is scarcely mentioned in the love letters to Trekkie. Adamson (2001) reminds the reader that up to the time that he started his *Autobiography* (1960), Leonard was assiduously editing Virginia's volumes of essays and her unpublished fiction and working on her diaries, thereby neglecting his own writing. None of this is discussed in the letters between Leonard and Trekkie.

In a letter of 1943, Woolf writes of his recurrent but transient feelings of abandonment when Trekkie was about to take
temporary leave of him to rejoin Ian: "You would never guess,
I believe, that every time you say, as you do, 'Well, goodbye,
Leonard' and look at me with the sternness—and at the same
time kindness which I like so much—before disappearing into
the Russell Square tube—that as I turn away I think of Thucydides, the greatest and most astringent of historians. The reason is that no one for the last 2500 years has succeeded in
giving a more perfect description of *that desert feeling* which
comes over me in Bernard Street than Thucydides: 'It is as
though *the spring had died out of the year*'"[24] (1901–69, 478;
emphasis added). For Leonard, to feel "that desert feeling"
meant coming back full circle to the desolation in childhood
he had experienced in the deserted family garden. (The dying
of spring evokes Persephone.)

Editing, Publishing, Journalism, and Writing

Amidst all his other tasks and duties (including looking after
Virginia, writing articles and books, publishing, editing, and
even doing menial jobs like typesetting for his Hogarth Press),
Woolf also worked as a journalist and editor for a number of
magazines. This culminated in his becoming editor of the literary part of the magazine published by Maynard Keynes called
Nation and Atheneum. Leonard started there in 1923 and stayed
on for eight years. He even wrote a weekly column about
books. He arranged for many leading British writers to do reviews, and he contributed his own articles and fiction. The
magazine was a success, and Woolf was much respected and

---

[24] Woolf speculated that this is what Thucydides "quoted" from Peri-
cles on his partings from Aspasia.

admired for his activity there.[25] Spotts (1989) says of Woolf's quality of work at Hogarth Press, "The works published by Hogarth Press are Leonard Woolf's greatest tangible legacy" (276). In addition to publishing books by Virginia, himself, and Freud and his followers at Hogarth Press, Leonard published works of Edmund Blunden, Isaac Bunin, Constantine Cavafy, Cecil Day Lewis, T. S. Eliot, E. M. Forster, Dostoevsky, Federico García Lorca, Thomas Hardy, Harold Nicolson, William Plomer, Herbert Read, Rilke, Bertrand Russell, Vita Sackville-West, Esther Salaman, H. G. Wells, Rebecca West, and many others.

Spotts (1989) observes that Woolf began writing as a boy and continued for the rest of his life: "In the intervening years he published two novels, four short stories, a play, more than thirty works of nonfiction, a five-volume autobiography, well over a thousand reviews and essays, dozens of pamphlets on international political questions and countless memoranda for the Labour Party and the Fabian Society. As manager of a publishing house, he read mountains of manuscripts and published more than a thousand of them, thirty-four printed by hand" (265).[26]

The Last Years

As a very old man (aged eighty-nine), he wondered about how valuable and useful his many seemingly productive years of

[25] Not the least of which was his editorial and publishing correspondence there (and at Hogarth Press), which amounted to about three thousand letters, according to Spotts (1989, 275).

[26] Woolf called himself "a socialist of a peculiar sort" (Spotts, 1989, 371). He had idiosyncratic views but usually allied himself with the left wing of the Labour party. He was of course anti-imperialist and anti-Nazi. His views on international government were expressed in a book of that title, published in 1916, which influenced the charters of both the League of Nations and the United Nations Organization.

political work and political writing had been. Was it worthwhile? He seems to feel he had had no choice: "It is in the pit
of my stomach as well as in the cooler regions of my brain that
I feel and think about what I see happening in the human ant-
heap around me, the historical and political events which seem
to me to make the difference between a good life and a bad, between civilization and barbarism. . . . All these excuses and explanations of why I have performed 200,000 hours of useless
work are no doubt merely another way of confessing that the
magnetic field of my own occupations produced the usual self-
deception, the belief that they were important" (Woolf 1969,
171, 172). But Woolf concludes, "Though all that I tried to do
politically was completely futile and ineffective and unimportant, for me personally it was right and important that I should
do it, even though at the back of my mind I was well aware that
it was ineffective and unimportant. To say this is to say that I
agree with what Montaigne, the first civilized modern man,
says somewhere: 'It is not the arrival, it is the journey which
matters'" (172). Before this statement, Woolf wrote, "I have no
doubt that, if at any moment I had become convinced that my
political work produced absolutely no effect at all in any direction, I would have stopped it altogether and have retired to cultivate my garden—the last refuge of disillusion" (171).

Gardening

Gardening was one of the greatest pleasures of the last years of
this wise old man. Spotts writes, "From 1940 onward, the physical and psychological center of Leonard's life was Monk's House
and especially its garden. There, daily life followed a regular
pace and pattern: "[gardening in the morning,] writing and
answering mail in the afternoons and reading in the evenings"
(1989, 469).

Woolf spent the last ten years of his life not only in passionately gardening, but occasionally traveling (both activities usually in the company of Trekkie Parsons), and he was writing the five volumes of his autobiography. Trekkie was as enthusiastic about gardening as he was; in the letters and the excerpts from their diaries[27] in Adamson's book there are scores of references to gardens and to flowers.[28] She made him happy, happier, he implies, than he had been with Virginia.[29] It is fascinating that gardens, the site of his childhood experiences of "cosmic unhappiness," play such a large part both in the letters between Leonard and Trekkie and in their lives. Leonard connects the anniversary of their emotional (and perhaps also sexual) closeness with a garden. He writes to her in October 1943 that he remembers "exactly the impression you made on me in Feb. [1942], the first time I came to tea. Your beauty and the beauty of your room and pictures, and your mind and moods appealed enormously to me, but I felt too that you were aloof from me in another world and that I had nothing to offer you. But you *haunted* me, *for some reason particularly with the flowers there and [the] garden, and that, I suppose, was what made me suddenly lay freesias on your doorstep*—a thing I had never thought of doing to anyone else" (93; emphasis added). The turning point in their relationship, he writes, was in October following their first meeting, when she consented, for the first time after their beginning to go out together, to go back home

---

[27] Trekkie started a diary late in life, perhaps motivated to compete with Virginia, whose diaries were being edited by Leonard for posthumous publication.

[28] In a rather desultory count, I found about 140 references to flowers and gardens in Adamson's (2001) collection of the couple's letters and of Trekkie's diary entries.

[29] One hopes she made him sexually happy as well in their long affair. Certainly his letters to her are intimate and amorous. Trekkie apparently destroyed part of their correspondence.

with him at the end of a date.[30] He is recalling the anniversary
of that October twentieth in the letter written approximately
one year later. This was the first time presumably that he
showed her and she saw his garden, and we do not know if that
could be a metaphor for whatever else they showed, saw, and
did. Their playful, affectionate, and often erotically charged
letters reveal that gardening together was characteristic of their
activities when they, for "half the week for the better part of
twenty-six years" (Adamson 2001), lived together in Leonard's
home.[31] Even when apart, their fantasy life featured wishing the
other were present, during which time each was made happy
by the sights and smells in gardens or among flowers. Their letters convincingly show him to have been at times almost ecstatically happy to love and feel loved by her. For example,
from a wartime letter of Leonard's (October 30, 1943):

> I have tried to keep this letter severely practical. . . .
> It is not romantic, though it may be dangerous, to
> love anyone like you as much as I love you. *It is ro-*
> *mantic to love someone passionately who isn't worth*
> *a passion—it's dangerous to love passionately some-*
> *one worth a passion—and the more worth the more*
> *dangerous. If ever anyone was worth a passion, dear-*
> *est, it's you.* Sometimes when I leave you a—I dare-
> say unreasonable—terror comes over me, that I shall
> weary, bore, annoy you and that the next time I see
> you I shall find that you can't tolerate me. I don't

---

[30] Their correspondence begins in 1941 but becomes frequent and intense only in 1943, falling off in the postwar years, when they were not much
apart except for Trekkie's many holidays with Ian.

[31] Adamson (2001) writes, "Their love was passionate and especially
during the war years erotically charged" (xxii).

really know why you should, particularly the ap-
palling insistence and persistence which I know I
possess and cannot control, which is due to some
horrible fire in my entrails and must be a weariness
of flesh and mind to other people. I had hoped that
age would put it out but I don't really think it does.[32]
It makes things obsess me. But only once before in
my life has it made a person obsess me. And it's because you are in every way so worthy of obsession
and passion, that my terrors are not unreasonable.
(94–95; emphasis added on what appears to be
an expression of the remains of a madonna/whore
complex)

The terrors (like those of childhood in the gardens) are of loss,
as he had lost Virginia (to whom he refers at the end of the
quote). Of course as a child it was the loss of his childhood and
the relationships with father and mother that he was afraid of.
He ends this passionate letter to Trekkie with a significant footnote: "I am beginning to enjoy Don Quixote. I like 'damsels
there were in times past that at the end of fourscore years old,
all which time they never slept one day under a roof, went as
entire and pure maidens to their graves as the very mother
who bore them'" (Adamson, 95). This delicious quote from
Cervantes ironically points out the idealization of, the need to
"virginize," mother.[33] Is Leonard's citing the denial of mother's
sexuality an unconscious revelation of the adult Leonard's
consummation of his sexual passion for Trekkie? He had at the
least found a woman who could really care about him and so,

[32] He was then sixty-three.
[33] Don Quixote, of course, never even spoke to, much less bedded, his
beloved, idealized slut, Dulcinea del Toboso.

one hopes, was no longer the boy who was terrified of mother's and father's sexuality. He literally worshiped Trekkie and, although she seems to have little of the dominatrix about her, his letters show a readiness for passivity as well as humility. He frequently addressed her in the letters as "Dearest Tiger"[34] (after Blake's "Tyger" poem) and even writes a humorous poem of sexual excitement in which he dares to aspire to her toe!:

> "To possess all of you, body, mind and soul,
> For in love there's nothing between nothing and the
> whole;
> I love your eyes, your mouth, your hand, your foot,
> your ear—"
> "Not quite so fast, not quite so fast my dear,
> You have no *locus standi,* no claims, I fear,
> No place or rights or privileges here."
> "Darling, of course I know
> That this is so;
> Mine was a cry
> For what's beyond the sky;
> On this low earth my claim is pretty low,
> You must allow,
> Only a toe"[35] (Adamson 2000, 129–30)

(This comic effusion does seem to evoke Don Quixote and his Dulcinea.) There is no confidence of taking sexual possession

[34] In response to "Dear Tiger" escalating to "Dearest of Tigers," Trekkie responded, "The tiger is too true and has always stalked about in me too ready to show its teeth and claws" (Adamson 2001, xvii).

[35] Kissing Virginia's and Trekkie's toes appears five or six times in Leonard's letters. His humility and masochism are strongly suggested, but could he also have been something of a foot fetishist?

in this surely ironic verse (for which Leonard apologized). But what people do sexually cannot be ascertained from what they write about.

Here is part of a letter of Leonard's following the one above—from 1944, after Ian had returned to England from France. It expresses the positive promise of the garden. He addresses Trekkie as "Darling Tiger, Luriana"[36] and continues:

> I think that even your toe (and even *your* toe) would have softened if it had been able to look into my heart when I turned the corner into the garden here on Thursday. For it would have seen how I missed and wanted you. It was as if a magician had waved a wand over the garden in the three days and completely changed it. All the daffodils, crown imperials, and hyacinths in full bloom. The plum trees white, in the greenhouse the freesias a mass of flowers and the great red buds of the great lily busting the sheath. But you have become so great a part of the garden and of me—no, not a part, but the whole . . . that I feel it's wrong when the flowers come out when you're not here. I simply don't want them without you. (120; note the toe metaphor)

Six months before these two letters he had written to her, "I must tell you that I love you though I think you know it, and that it is a twilight world without you" (Adamson 2001, 98). The expressions of fervent mutual love in the correspondence continue, but the passionate intensity wanes a bit toward the end—not surprising considering Leonard's extreme old age—

---

[36] Luriana is a reference to a flower from a poem they both liked.

although the affection remains. His last letter to her when she was away on one of her trips with Ian in 1968 was addressed to "Dearest" and ended with "Love from your Leonard" (301). Trekkie's last letter to him starts with "Dearest" and ends with "Tons of love" (303–04). When he had a stroke in April 1969, he initially suffered from aphasia, but he recovered enough to be able finish the proofs of his last book and occasionally to go out into the garden. Adamson says that in the months following his stroke Trekkie "rarely left his side" (304). Leonard gradually grew weaker and died in August 1969.[37]

Leonard Woolf was never interested in power; he did not seek success. He had a strong ethical sense, like his father, and although he achieved success in many fields, he centered his achievements on ideas and the writing of books dedicated to the improvement of political and economic conditions. He was an achiever as a civil servant and magistrate in Ceylon; a journalist; an editor; a publisher; a writer; and, perhaps above all, as the protector and guardian of his genius wife and her writings.[38]

Spotts remarks, "[Leonard Woolf's] goal was not public esteem but a personal sense of having produced something innately worthwhile" (1989, 9). Spotts quotes E. M. Forster, Woolf's friend from the time they were fellow students at Cambridge, who said of Leonard, "What a life he has led, and how well he has led it" (ix).

Haunted by Mother?

Perhaps Leonard gradually grew to feel, after the death of Virginia and during the decades shared with Trekkie and Ian, that

---

[37] Ian died in 1980 and Trekkie in 1995.

[38] He also once ran for Parliament, and here he lost; he came in third of three, which was no surprise to him

he was no longer the family member who was less loved than the others. In the fourth volume of his autobiography (1967), Woolf reports the death of his mother in 1939. This is followed by a restatement of his conviction that his mother disliked him (which he had already expressed in his first volume [1960]). In the later book he also repeats his conviction that he resembles his father and the Woolf side of the family rather than his mother's: "I was very much my father's and very little my mother's son, and there were many sides of my character and mind which were unsympathetic to my mother; I had no patience with her invincible, optimistic sentimentality, and my unsentimentality, which seemed to her hardness and harshness, distressed her. There was no quarrel or rift between us, and I always went to see her once a week or once a fortnight up to the day of her death—but, though she would not have admitted it herself, I was, I think, her *least-loved* child" (253–54). The "less-loved" by mother, written at eighty-one when he was describing his unhappy childhood, has, in the later book at eighty-seven, been negatively enhanced to "least-loved." The octogenarian was furnishing evidence, with this negative augmentation, that—despite his conscious intentions and the good feelings and transcendent functioning in his old age (all these intermittently but significantly present for a large part of his life)[39]—he had been living out, affirming in negation as it were, the childhood fantasy and fearful conviction that there was no life without mother.

Yet he ended his autobiography, and I will end this chapter, with an expression of the transcendence of the "cosmic unhappiness" of the motherless child in the dirty, deserted garden

[39] Especially during his life with Trekkie after the deaths of his mother and Virginia.

that shadowed his early life. At the end of the last volume of his autobiography, finished in the year that he died, he writes,

> There are other assets of old age. The storms and stresses of life, the ambitions and competitions are over. The futile and unnecessary and false responsibilities have fallen from one's shoulders and one's conscience. Even the false proverbs tend to become true for old people, for instance, that it is no good crying over spilt milk—after the age of eighty. One has learnt the lesson that sufficient for the day is the good thereof. And one can *almost* say:
>   Grow old along with me!
>   The best is yet to be,
>   The last of life, for which the first was made.
> And one can say again: "It is the *journey,* not the arrival, which matters." (1960, 210; emphasis added)

The quotation from Browning is surely addressed to Trekkie, whose love helped (or perhaps "*almost*" helped) exorcise his parental ghosts and had made Woolf's "journey" such a happy one toward its end.

The Final Return to the Garden

After his cremation, Leonard Woolf's ashes were buried under a tree—beside the place that he had buried Virginia's—in the garden.[40]

---

[40] Of Monk's House, the country home he lived in for so many years with Virginia and alone or with Trekkie after Virginia's death.

X

A Third Literary Example—
Sergei Timofeevich Aksakov

Verily, in adversity, the worst unhappiness
is to have been happy.
—*Boethius,* Consolation of Philosophy, *book 2 (anno 523?)*

S ergei Timofeevich Aksakov, a Russian author much admired and popular in his own country but not widely
read outside Russia these days, was born in 1791, in Ufa,
near the Siberian border. He died in 1859. His father,
Timofei Stepanovich Aksakov, was a minor legal official whose
ancestors were from the lesser nobility. His mother, Maria
Nicolaevna, had a lower-class background; her father achieved
a self-made success and became a wealthy, important civic
official in Ufa.

Aksakov is the oldest of the great nineteenth-century Rus-

sian writers, eight years older than Alexander Pushkin (1799–
1837) and eighteen years older than Aksakov's friend Nikolai
Gogol (1809–52). After Pushkin, Mikhail Lermontov (1814–41),
and then Gogol died, Aksakov was for some years regarded
as Russia's greatest living writer.[1] He is now known chiefly for
his slightly disguised autobiographical writings—three books
about the lives of his grandparents and parents and his own
childhood and youth. Aksakov's reputation as a great author
stemmed from these memoirs. Remembering and describing
the conflict-laden ambivalent relationship between his parents
and his paternal grandparents and between the two partners
of each couple brought out Aksakov's gifts for psychological
observation. He also had a special talent for the description of
nature. Crankshaw (1982) writes in his introduction to Aksakov's first volume of memoirs,

> I have left [his pictures of nature] until last, partly
> because it is in his treatment of the natural world
> that Aksakov's genius is most immediately and evi-
> dently apparent, partly because it is above all in his
> exact descriptions of the Russian landscape, the
> Russian seasons (the torrential coming of spring;
> the ice-bound winter days; the killing heat of har-
> vest time), the intimate, shimmering, multitudinous
> life of birds, beasts, butterflies, fish that I find my-
> self thinking of Aksakov when he is not at hand.
> And the whole, everything he sees and describes, is

[1] Ivan Turgenev (1818–83), like Gogol a friend of Aksakov, published
his first book, *A Sportsman's Sketches*, in 1852; Leo Tolstoy (1828–1910) was
just starting to publish in 1851; Fyodor Dostoyevsky (1821–81) had published
Poor Folk in 1846. But all three of these great writers did not publish the novels that guaranteed their reputations until the 1860s.

true and real down to the last ruffled feather of a
bird at odds with the wind, the uneven ring of a
horse-shoe that has lost a nail, the creak and rumble
of an unsprung waggon. Nothing is abstract. Nothing is generalized. (xiv)

He was aided by a marvelous memory, apparently an almost lifelong talent that showed itself very early but func-
tioned intermittently. It only became fully operative, in a spon-
taneous and involuntary way that resembled Proust's, when
he was writing his memoirs in late middle age (see Salaman
1973). At three he claimed he recalled being weaned and other
very early events that his parents said he was never told about.
As an old man, Aksakov remembered that when he was five
he was able to tell his recollections of his illnesses and his trav-
els to his three-year-old sister. It is remarkable, and relevant to
this book, that in spite of his great gift of memory, he was as
an adult unable to remember the spring season (a time he
loved so extravagantly all his life) from his seventh to his fif-
teenth years. He had been sent away from home to school at
eight. I believe it was for him the cruelty of the intense promise of spring, associated with the turning point in his life that
school represented in relation to the physical separation from
his mother, which determined this amnesia. The early years
with mother contained the happiness that recalling in subsequent adversity is so cruel, about which I have quoted Boethius
and Dante.

In his 1852 book on hunting birds (the second of his published books) he wrote, "I must repeat a little of what I said in
the Foreword to my *Notes on Fishing:* my little book is neither
a treatise on shooting nor a natural history of all forms of game.
My book is no more and no less than the simple notes of a pas-

sionate hunter and observer: sometimes quite full and detailed, sometimes superficial and one-sided, but always written in good conscience. Russia has many hunters, and I do not doubt they will be well disposed. Learned naturalists may fully rely on my words. *I never present suppositions as fact and assert nothing that I have not witnessed with my own eyes"* (1852, 4; emphasis added).

I think something of the impressive good character of the man, featuring a passionate attachment to telling the truth of his experiences as best he could (noted by so many commentators), comes through in this disclaimer. And, to judge from his writings, it seems to be accurate. His first biographical book (1856) has his grandfather Stepan Mikhailovich Aksakov as its central, unforgettable figure. Sergei did remember him vividly, but the grandfather died when the boy was five, and the author is obviously writing principally about what he has been told—in large part, I conjecture, told by his intelligent and literate mother. And yet, his convincing descriptions of the thoughts and actions of his parents as he outlines their complex, conflict-ridden relationship often read more like fiction than memoir. He tells the reader their thoughts and feelings; the fictionalizing would appear to be a combination of what he has heard, modified by his wise impressions and views of the people who informed him. He also felt at first that he needed to disguise his family story by his idiosyncratic method of making memoir sound like fiction. Later, when the censorship lightened after the death of Czar Nicholas I, Aksakov changed some of the names of the family members and of the family estates back to the originals. But Aksakov was not at ease as a writer of fiction and did not regard it as his métier. In a letter written late in his life, he wrote, "People close to me have heard more than once that I am lacking in free creativeness, that I can only write standing on the ground of reality, following a thread of a true event; that all my attempts of the other kind turned out unsatisfactory and have convinced me that I do not possess the gift of pure invention" (Aksakov, quoted in Salaman [1973, 23]).

Aksakov was his mother's firstborn son. (Maria Nicolaevna had previously given birth to a daughter. She was ecstatically preoccupied with her first child and felt devastated when the four-month-old died suddenly.) The boy who replaced her was a sickly child. Sergei, who, the doctors warned, also might die, quickly became his mother's precious darling. She nursed him tenderly and tirelessly, so that as a child he became completely dependent on her. Sergei remained the favorite of her children until he moved to Moscow as a man and dared to get married. He writes of his early childhood, "The constant presence of my mother is part of every recollection I have. Her image makes an inseparable part of my own existence, and therefore it is not prominent in the scattered pictures of my earliest childhood, although invariably a part of them" (1858, 2).

Sergei's mother was young, beautiful, intelligent, and full of life. She could also be willful and stubborn. The boy was passionately attached to her. It seems clear from Aksakov's description that the closeness between mother and son in his early years when he was so ill resulted in the much-loved and overprotected, perceptive, and sensitive boy becoming her confidant.[2]

The doctors for years continued to predict that the child would die. The mother's persistent care helped save him, but it

---

[2] "My mother was my constant companion," he writes of his later childhood (Aksakov 1856b, 10).

also made for a strong masochistic dependency that provided
Sergei with an unconscious motive to remain sick that preserved that dependency. The boy developed a deep and persistent interest in sick, hurt, and ill-used animals and people.
In his story of his grandfather, he illustrates his masochism, and
its connection with his longing for his childhood, when, in his
midfifties, he writes about the curtains of homemade muslin
that served as mosquito netting around the beds in his grandfather's house. The netting was

> indispensable; without it, the wicked mosquitoes
> would have kept [grandfather] awake and devoured
> him. Those winged musicians swarmed round the
> bed, each driving its long proboscis into the fine
> fabric which protected him, and kept up their mo-
> notonous serenade all through the night. It sounds
> absurd, but I cannot conceal *the fact that I like the
> shrill high note and even the bite of the mosquito* for
> it reminds me of sleepless nights on the banks of
> the Buguruslan [river], where the bushes grew thick
> and green and all around the nightingales called;
> and I remember the beating heart of youth and that
> vague feeling, *half pleasure and half pain,* for which
> I would now give up all that remains of the sinking
> fire of life. (1856a, 19; emphasis added)

Aksakov became, like his mother, oversensitive and over-
reactive to any form of injustice or brutality or to weakness and
suffering in others. Here is some of what he documents of his
ardent involvement with his little sister and with animals that
followed the recovery from his childhood near-fatal illness:

When I began to recover, my feelings of pity for all
suffering became morbid and excessive. The first
object of this feeling was my little sister: I could not
bear to see her tears nor hear her cry without beginning at once to cry myself; she too was unwell at
that time. . . . Recovery was slow, and it was long
before I could walk. I lay whole days in my crib with
my sister beside me, amusing her with different toys
or by showing her pictures. Later I began to creep
about and to sit at the window which opened directly *onto the garden*. Birds of all kinds, even sparrows, were a great attraction and pleasure to me.
My mother . . . at once got me a cage and a pair of
pigeons, which passed their nights under my crib. I
have been told that my enchantment with my pets
was so great and expressed in such a manner that it
was impossible not to be infected by the sight of my
joy. (1858, 6; emphasis added)

The garden motif will return later in this chapter.

When he was a child and adolescent, Sergei was in many
ways more important to Maria than her husband or her five
other children. She had never been able to communicate in any
emotional depth with her well-meaning but unempathic, naive,
and somewhat dull husband. Aksakov both identified with his
mother's point of view and yet was eventually able to—perhaps
to preserve his identity *had* to—stand aside and view her, and
his father and grandparents, with what appears to be remarkable objectivity. For example, here is how Aksakov deals with
his mother's thoughts (but they are obviously his own relatively "objective" projections onto her views) in the first (1856a)

book of memoirs. The young girl is reacting to Timofei's (called Alexei in the book) proposal:

> She was considered a marvel of beauty and intelligence. Her suitor was certainly pretty in a boyish way—which was no recommendation to [her]—but rather simple and stupid, and passed with everyone for a plain country lad. She was quick and enterprising: he was timid and slow. She was educated and might almost be called learned, had read much, and had a wide range of intellectual interests; he was quite ignorant, had read nothing but a few silly novels and a song-book, and cared for little beyond snaring quails and flying his hawks. She was witty and tactful and shone in society; he could not string three words together; clumsy, shy, abject, and ridiculous, he could only blush and bow and squeeze into a corner or against a door, to escape from the talkative and sociable young men whom he positively feared, though he was in truth far cleverer than many of them. She had a firm, positive, unbending temper; he was humble and wanting in energy, easily silenced and easily discomfited. Was he the man to support and defend his wife in society and in domestic life? (94–95)[3]

Later Life

After he grew up and finished his education, Aksakov at sixteen left his provincial home and worked as a translator and

[3] Objectivity could not prevent Aksakov from being haunted by parents, but it ameliorated the haunting.

later as a press censor for the imperial Russian government, first in Petersburg and then in Moscow, where he lived for most of his adult life.[4] He retired from government service in 1839, aged forty-eight. (By then he had inherited wealth from his paternal grandfather and great aunt and did not need his salary.) Aksakov married at twenty-five and fathered fourteen children (nine survived); two of his sons (also writers) became well-known Slavophiles, and another became an important government official.

Aksakov had strong intellectual interests and many literary friends. For ten years he occasionally left Moscow and went to the country to manage his (formerly his grandfather's) estate near Siberia, but on returning to Moscow in 1836 (aged forty-seven), he bought an estate just outside that city, where he lived for the rest of his life. There he often acted as host to literary and artistic luminaries. His health deteriorated in later life, and he developed complete blindness in one eye and partial blindness in the other.[5] He then had to dictate his writings. The last months of his life were spent in blindness, in pain, and confined to his bed.

Aksakov's Writing

Aksakov in his early forties began earning money by writing for a Moscow journal. He had wanted to be an author for a good part of his life, but at first just dabbled in writing. He was profoundly fascinated by acting in and writing for the theater; this interest had begun in his school years. As a young man, he did a few translations of plays from the French (Molière, a French

---

[4] Readers of the *Memoir* volumes, which concentrate so much on childhood and youth in the provinces, may find this surprising.

[5] His mother also became blind years before she died.

edition of Sophocles, etc.), tried not too successfully to write some plays of his own, and did brief critical theatrical reviews for periodicals. He made no attempt at serious writing until he began to write about his parents and paternal grandparents in 1840, when he was a middle-aged man of about fifty. Two fragments (as he later called his first memoir chapters) were published in a Moscow magazine in 1846. He really only became a kind of professional and a serious author during the last fifteen years of his life, after the family had lost much of their fortune.

His published writings in magazines were admired, and he was encouraged by their favorable reception to publish his first book, which was about fishing (1846). He then produced a similar book on hunting (1852). These two volumes in turn were much appreciated and not only by the reading public; Gogol and Turgenev praised them highly. Both men subsequently became friends of Aksakov, and he grew to be especially close to Gogol.[6] After Aksakov began to publish his memoirs, Gogol urged him to continue with his history of his family and go on to his own life story.

From 1846 on, Aksakov (who had become blind in one eye the year before) worked on his memoirs in a desultory way, and the entire first book of memoirs was not published until 1856 (when Aksakov was sixty-five). The initial family book, called in its English translations *A Family Chronicle* or *A Russian Gentleman* (1856a), is chiefly about his grandparents and his parents, and it ends with his own birth. It very quickly became even more popular than the short books on fishing and on hunting. Aksakov then, later in 1856, brought out the story of his school and college days, *A Russian Schoolboy* (1856b). His

---

[6] When he lived in the Moscow area, Aksakov hosted many literary celebrities, and Alexander Pushkin, Vissarion Belinski, and many lesser-known writers were also his friends and acquaintances.

last-published autobiographical volume, *Years of Childhood, or The Childhood of the Bagrov Grandson*, describes Aksakov's early childhood, the time in between the other two books;[7] it came out in 1858, a year before Aksakov died. A book of reminiscences of Gogol was published posthumously.

Aksakov's popular books, *Notes on Fishing* and *Notes of a Provincial Wildfowler*, were written during the time when he was also working at writing the family memoirs. Aksakov was adept at descriptions of both nature and human character. Gogol is alleged to have written Aksakov about his first two books that "your birds and fishes are more real than my men and women" (see Bayley 1974). Both nature books show a wonderful gift for minute descriptions of specific species and their habits and of specific kinds of landscapes and waters, all told in a prose whose beauty and preciseness of detail come through even in English translation. I will give some short examples of his observations and comments:

> The snipe begin to drum, twisting and turning in the blue spring heavens, plummeting from on high in a steep arc, and soaring sharply up again. (1852, 9)

[In a footnote, Aksakov comments,]

> The snipe is popularly known as "the wild sheep," because as it plunges vertically downward it partly folds one wing while flapping the other so hard that the wind resistance produces a sound like that of a lamb bleating. (293)

[7] The memoirs started out with the name Aksakov replaced by Bagrov, but by the last volume the author was using his own name and that of the family estate, Aksakovo.

Another example: Aksakov describes, in great detail, five different kinds of marshlands inhabited in spring by marshland birds. His categories are loose, and he makes it clear how each can vary. For example, he says of his second category, "dry marshland,"

"Dry marshland" is the name given to land that bears all the hallmarks of having earlier been fenland: tussocks, sometimes of enormous size, traces of dried-up springs, and various species of marsh grass, now interspersed with meadow species. For the most part such land becomes overgrown with bushes, being unsuitable for hay-making. It is quite usual for wet marshes and swamps to turn into dry marshland, as springs dry up along with the sources of streamlets, but I have sometimes witnessed the reverse process: dry marshes, which for decades have been a sorry sight to behold, reverting to swamp and fen. This occurs mostly when a long, wet autumn so saturates the ground that it can absorb no more moisture, and sudden frosts ensue, followed by very heavy snowfalls, followed by a wet spring. The long-dry springs reopen, the whole area is soaked by the rising groundwater, and a dead marsh is returned to life; the meadow grasses are gone within a year, and in a few years the bushes and trees die too. (19)

The man who called himself "a passionate hunter and observer" (1852, 4) ends his classification of marshlands with a paean to spring and its promise: "Such are the types of marsh that I am familiar with. The best of them is the open marsh—

meadowland with scattered bushes and trees, which floods in spring. How wonderful this can be on a warm spring morning! When the water level has fallen, leaving wet patches and little crests of black soil deposited from the fields, vegetation thrives as nowhere else. The sun heats the moist, heavy soil, and seems to draw grass and flowers out of it: you can almost see them growing! The bushes and trees are coming out, and their leaves are coated with a scented sheen. Every bush, every tree is wrapped in its own envelope of fragrant air" (23).[8] These are observations of a man who has been there and is reporting (with rapture) what he has seen and come to know.

Aksakov has an equally wonderful gift for psychological observation. Here is a short example of Aksakov's psychological acumen from his first book of memoirs. He is writing about the bad reception his mother had from her future sisters-in-law when it was announced that their brother intended to marry her. They set up complicated schemes to prejudice their paternalistic tyrant of a father against the marriage choice of his only son and heir:

> It is a well-known fact that in the good old days of the Empress Catherine—perhaps it is the case still—there was little love lost between a man's wife and his sisters; and the case was worse when the sisters had only one brother, because his wife must become the sole and undisputed mistress of the household. A great deal of selfishness underlies human nature; it works without our knowledge, and no one is exempt from it; honorable and kind people,

---

[8] Here April does not sound like the cruelest month. See below, however, for my speculation on the reason for Aksakov's not being able to remember the springs of his later boyhood.

not recognizing selfish motives in themselves, quite honestly attribute their actions to other and more presentable causes; but they deceive themselves and others unintentionally. Where there is no kindness of heart or refinement of manners, selfishness shows itself without any concealment or apology; and so it was with the *womenfolk* of [my grandfather]. (1856a, 77; emphasis added)[9]

The Memoirs

I am going to try to go through Aksakov's recollections in more or less chronological order; this will involve some repetition. His evocation of his paternal grandfather, Stepan Mikhailovich Aksakov, presents the reader with an unforgettable personality from the time of the empress Catherine the Great. Sergei Timofeevitch was only five when his grandfather died, but his memory and influence continued to dominate the subsequent family history.[10] Stepan Mikhailovich, strong and full of energy, ruled his estates, serfs, and family with despotic authority. The patriarch could read and write but was not well educated. He came from an ancient line of nobility but lived as a provincial country squire. Stepan Mikhailovich had the proverbial will (as well as whim) of iron. As a young man, he sold the lands he had inherited and moved his family, stock, and hundreds of serfs to the relatively unsettled eastern province of

---

[9] Although Chekhov's *The Three Sisters* was written over fifty years later, it contains a memorable depiction of the power an only brother's new (and also, like some of the "womenfolk" in Aksakov's *Memoirs*, nasty) wife could bring to bear on her husband to compromise his sisters' right to the parental home.

[10] Aksakov was haunted by grandparents as well as by parents.

Orenberg, close to Siberia. It was a pioneer venture in a land populated by tribes of Bashkir natives from whom he bought hundreds of acres for a small sum. He built and prospered. Stepan Mikhailovich had a complicated and contradictory nature. He was capable of kindness and compassion, but he was also stubborn, willful, and given to occasional outbursts of fury. He would behave, following these tantrums, as if they had never occurred. Nevertheless, he was highly respected because of his honesty and straightforwardness. His intimidated but often hostile and provocative wife usually had no choice but to give in to his wishes and fancies, yet she also sometimes stubbornly resisted his desires, usually with stealth and secrecy. In these conspiracies she had the frightened and often agitation-enhancing help of three of her four daughters. The old man was cleverer than everyone else and usually saw through their evasions and schemes. Drama and turmoil were repetitive occurrences.

Everyone in the household was terrified of the grandfather's rages and bad moods, but he was also loved and trusted. He looked out for his serf peasants and servants in his paternalistic way. His only son, Timofei Stepanovich Aksakov, the author's father, was a rather passive, relatively uneducated, self-doubting, tenderhearted, good-looking man who was astounded that his future wife—a brilliant, educated, beautiful, and popular young woman—would even consider his wish to marry her.[11]

Aksakov's Childhood

Aksakov, writing of the attachments of his childhood, first mentions that he had a wet nurse who "loved me passionately" (1858,

[11] He was a man that she probably thought she could dominate. She had more power, intelligence, and force, but he was willful and apparently took revenge in her later years as a wife by taking mistresses.

1). As an old man he tells the reader he has early memories of
her kissing and crying over him. And in his later childhood,
the peasant woman, now a serf working for another master,
would walk twenty miles each Saturday evening to reach him
at Ufa on Sunday morning simply to see her former charge,
then start back to be able to work for her owner the next day.
In the story of his childhood, Aksakov next mentions his great
love for his three-years-younger sister. He then goes on to describe his mother's passionate attachment to him as her firstborn son, her remarkable devotion increased by the long, serious illness that made the doctors despair for his life. That her
first child had been a girl so disappointed and enraged her fa-
ther-in-law (Stepan Mikhailovich), who had characteristically
assumed that his wish for a male child to continue his line would
be granted, that he did not want to see the child.[12] When Sergei
was born, the new grandfather (his narcissistic injury now as-
suaged) was eager to greet his grandson. But, years later when
the boy was five, Stepan Mikhailovich was less than pleased
with Sergei when his parents visited the grandparents and he
and his little sister were left in their care. Sergei's mother, accompanied by her husband, needed to go on to Kazan, the
province's largest city (250 miles away) to seek out a cure for a
severe illness that had followed another of her pregnancies. The
boy felt afraid of his dominating and disapproving grandfather,
and he was desolate at the separation from both parents. Most
of all, the perceptive child, sensing how ill his mother was, felt
terrified by the possibility that she might never return. So his
first remembered impressions of the grandfather and of his estate, Aksakovo, were intensely negative. His grandfather was

---

[12] Maria Nicolaevna had been so enraptured with motherhood that
she did not even notice this.

openly scornful of the boy, calling him a crybaby. But after his grandfather's death when the boy was five, Sergei felt guilty and confused and, in his ambivalence, was tormented by the loss of that powerful paternal presence. The boy subsequently came to love Aksakovo, where, after the death of Stepan Mikhailovich, his family moved to live with his grandmother. It was at Aksakovo that he learned to fish and to hunt.

Aksakov's Formal Education

When the boy was eight, he and his parents left Aksakovo in Orenberg province to go again to Kazan, this time to visit some friends of his father's. The friend suggested to Timofei Stepanich that Sergei be left in Kazan to go to school there. The school offered better educational prospects than could be found near the family estate, but apparently the suggestion was primarily motivated by the friend's observations of and reaction to the all too obvious closeness between the boy and his mother. Aksakov reconstructs the comments of the man from Kazan: "Do take a piece of friendly advice and send Seryozha to the grammar school here. It is especially important, because I can see he is his mother's darling, and she will spoil him and coddle him till she makes an old woman of him" (1856b, 5).

Maria Nicolaevna did not take kindly to the intimation that she was interfering with the boy's masculinity, and she strongly protested: "My mother turned pale at the thought of parting with her treasure, and replied, with much agitation, that I was still young and weak in health (which was true, to some extent) and so devoted to her that she could not make up her mind in a moment to such a change. As for me, I sat there more dead than alive, neither hearing nor understanding anything further that was said" (Aksakov 1856b, 5).

In response to the father's taking the friend's suggestion seriously, both mother and son began to sob. The mother insisted that she and Sergei were not ready for the separation. The boy's going to school in Kazan was postponed for a year, and, Aksakov writes, "I began once more my life of blissful happiness in my mother's company" (7).

As an old man Aksakov writes another hosanna to his childhood as epitomized by his happiness in the spring of that particular year when he was back with his mother: "Ah, where is it now, that magic world, the fairy tale of human life, which so many grown-up people treat roughly and rudely, shattering its enchantment by ridicule or premature enlightenment? The happiness of childhood is the Golden Age, and the recollection of it has power to move the old man's heart with pleasure *and with pain*. Happy the man who once possessed it and is able to recall the memory of it in later years! With many that time passes by unnoticed or unenjoyed; and all that remains in the ripeness of age is the recollection of the coldness or even *cruelty* of men" (1856b, 8–9; emphasis added). (The passage underlines the pleasure of spring[13] and childhood but also alludes to the concomitant pain and cruelty of the recollections of happiness in a later time of misery [referred to in the quotations from Boethius and Dante]. References to the evocation of the loss of past bliss evoked by the promise of spring have been strewn throughout this book [cf. T. S. Eliot's beginning lines from "The Waste Land."]).

Summer followed spring, and Aksakov writes of the resumption of joy in his mother's company: "I spent the whole summer in the intoxication of a child's happiness, and suspected nothing" (9). During this respite, Sergei's mother tried

---

[13] An idealized spring here clearly stands for an idealized childhood.

to convince the boy and herself that he needed to go away to school. She zealously wanted her son to have a good education and yet could not bear the thought of separation. Her ambivalence was extreme. Sergei clung to her desperately, and she was his "constant companion."

And yet Maria Nicolaevna also undertook to prepare her son for his entrance examinations; she dreaded that his failing these would put the family to shame. His reading and writing improved rapidly under her tutelage, and the boy reviewed and improved on the arithmetic his father had taught him. Aksakov wrote that she eventually convinced him of "the advantages that the educated have over the ignorant, and I was able to understand her. She was remarkably intelligent and had unusual powers of expression; she could speak what was in her mind with a passion that was hard to resist, and her influence over me was absolute and supreme. At last she inspired me with such courage, such zeal to carry out her darling wish as soon as possible and justify her hopes, that I looked forward even with impatience to our journey to Kazan" (1856b, 10–11). The closeness to, and identification with, his mother in relation to reading and literature led to Sergei's lifelong passionate attachment to books. During this summer at Aksakovo he actively repeated his mother's role as tutor by teaching his beloved younger sister to read. (He had previously read his favorite books to her.)[14]

As the summer waned, after more than a year of Sergei's predominant denial of the impending separation, the periods of "blissful happiness" (7) in his mother's company gave way to a persistent anticipatory terror of separation and loss. He

[14] This gift to his beloved sister was also a holding onto his mother by identification with her.

writes, "I submitted with an aching heart to the destiny that awaited me. . . . Only my love for my mother increased so much as actually to frighten her" (9). The boy became more depressed and withdrawn: "I would not go one step [from mother's] side. When she tried to send me out to play or look at my pigeons and hawks, I refused to go anywhere and always gave the same answer, 'I don't want to, mamma'" (10). This was a longing for, and a reenactment of, the earlier time of his illness, "when for whole years she had never left my bedside; when she slept, no one knew—and no hand but hers was suffered to touch me" (11).

Breakdown and Return of Illness

The boy was finally taken by his parents to be left at the boarding school in Kazan. There he suffered a physical and mental breakdown. This began a few days after Sergei moved into the school.

The boy and his father had visited the doctor assigned by the school, who "issued a certificate of health and bodily vigour" (13). On returning to his mother, the boy noticed that she had been weeping. Aksakov wrote as an old man, "My father eagerly reported all that had happened to us. My mother looked at me with an expression [that] I shall never forget, even if I have still a hundred years to live. She took me in her arms and said, 'You are my happiness, you are my pride!' What more could I ask? In my own way, I was proud and happy too, and took courage" (1856b, 13).

But then, several days later, Maria Nicolaevna visited Sergei in school and for the first time saw her son with his hair cut short and wearing the school uniform: "She failed to recognize me at the first moment, threw up her hands, cried out, and fell fainting to the floor. I cried out wildly and fell at her feet. . . . My mother's swoon, which lasted for half an hour, terrified my father" (15).

The boy's fainting, I speculate, represented a sudden identification, under stress, with the fallen woman; the son transiently becoming or merging with his mother. This sequence precedes his subsequent repetitive attacks of fainting, which were diagnosed, and probably misdiagnosed, as epilepsy (the "falling sickness"). There seems little doubt that it was hysterical epilepsy.

Following this dramatic encounter, Maria returned to the school to see Sergei every day, even several times a day. The boy's agitation increased and, on the advice of the school officials, who told Maria Nicolaevna that her visits were injuring her son's health, she reluctantly yet abruptly ceased her multiple daily visits. The boy felt devastated. And then, again *suddenly,* at the insistence of the school authorities, she left for home with her husband with no warning and without even saying goodbye. She had previously promised the boy she would see him again at the school before they separated. Aksakov wrote, "But there is one thing that still puzzles me—how she could make up her mind to play a trick on me. Before dinner she told me that she would leave the next day or the day after, and that we should meet twice more; she said too that she was spending that evening with [our friends], and would not visit me. To depart secretly and without saying good-by—that was an unlucky idea urged by [the school people]. Of course, they wished to spare us both, and me especially, the pain of a final parting; but their calculation was not verified. Even now I am convinced that this well-meant deception had many sad results" (17–18).

The mother's betrayal in his boyhood still burned in the old man's memory as he wrote. Sergei's response to his mother's farewell letter, delivered after she had departed, was to go into a kind of catatonic state, accompanied by heart palpitations. The mother's anxiety and remorse led her to return to the school after a few days. The school officials at first refused to let her take the boy out of the school to where she was staying, but finally they were convinced they ought to do so. Aksakov wrote, "The first moment of our meeting it is impossible for me to describe; but *never in my after-life did I experience a thrill of happiness to compare with that.* For some minutes we were silent and only wept for joy. But this did not last for long and the thought of coming separation soon drove all other thoughts and feelings from me, and made my heart ache" (1856b, 21; emphasis added). There can be no doubt of the eight-year-old's urgent terrible feelings evoked by the threat of separation from his mother.

Maria blamed herself for having deceived the boy. She had fainted again as her sledge had left Kazan, and finally she insisted on returning alone. After being with her for a blissful and then tearful overnight, the boy went back to the school and the mother returned to Aksakovo, first promising to come back to see him as soon as the roads became passable in spring.[15]

At first Sergei was miserable, but he gradually became interested in schoolwork and began to adjust to the school routine. He was "placed on the top bench in all subjects, side by side with the best scholars" (26). This increased the envy and hostility of the other students. Then he again suffered a series of hysterical fits of fainting and seeming catatonia and was taken to the hospital.[16] He was given medicine of some kind and im-

---

[15] "The spring thaws made travelling impossible for a time" (22).

[16] "Hysterical fits accompanied by such violent weeping and sobbing that I lost consciousness for some minutes; and I was told later that at such times the muscles of my face were convulsed" (31).

proved a bit. His body servant, Yefrem Yevséich, who had been left with Sergei and had promised Maria he would let her know if her son became ill, wrote "with no precautions and without due regard to the facts" (36) that his young master had epilepsy and was in the hospital.

There was rumor that he was "catching the black sickness" (32), that is, epilepsy: "The next day . . . I felt a sudden severe oppression on the chest, and a few minutes later burst out sobbing, and then fell senseless on the floor. . . . In the evening there was a severe fit which lasted much longer" (32–33).

The Past Recaptured

Aksakov writes about his fits, "Like everyone else, I believed at the time that no cause could be assigned for the coming-on of these fits, but now I am convinced of the contrary; they were always produced by some *sudden* recollection of that past life which presented itself to me in a moment with all the liveliness and clarity of dreams at night" (34; emphasis added). These moments consisted of

> sights and sounds. . . . When I was thinking of something quite different, even when I was entirely taken up by my lessons, *suddenly* the sound of someone's voice, probably like some voice I had heard before, or a patch of sunlight on wall or window, such as had once before thrown light in just the same way upon objects dear and familiar, or a fly buzzing and beating against the panes as I had often watched them do when I was a child, [made me] instantly and for one instant, though no consciousness could detect the process, recall the forgotten past and gave

a shock to my overstrung nerves. . . .[17] Thus I was
saying a lesson one day, when *suddenly* a pigeon
perched on the window-sill and began to turn round
and coo; at once I thought of my pet pigeons at
home, and the oppression on my chest came on immediately and was followed by a fit. (34–35; emphasis added)

It is uncanny that even the prose style here sounds like Proust's
long, convoluted sentences (written on a similar theme so many
decades later), as Aksakov is detailing the sensory impressions
that brought on for him—as for Proust and his hero, Marcel—
moments of such intensity as to abolish the passage of time.[18]
But Aksakov's "Proustian" moments of dreamlike intensity are
nightmare versions of the great French novelist's rapturous in-
stances of "The Past Recaptured."[19] The sudden connections of
present and past again evoked in Sergei another instance of recalling happiness in the midst of misery.

On receiving the news from Yevséich that Sergei was in
the hospital suffering from epilepsy, Maria Nicolaevna started
immediately for Kazan, despite roads declared to be impassable
due to the spring thaw. At a flooding river, the villagers refused
to take her across; she hired some fishermen who, after a frost,
somehow got her, by foot (!), across the precariously iced-over
river, which she had been told was impossible to traverse. She

[17] Cf. the "And Suddenly Phenomena."

[18] One recalls Proust's lifelong longing for his mother's goodnight kiss
from childhood that begins, and resounds throughout, *The Remembrance of
Things Past*. (Proust's is a great example of someone haunted by parents, but
to do justice to his ambivalent hauntings, as I originally intended to do,
would overload this book.)

[19] The rapture basically stems from his guilt-ridden wish to go back to
the instance of his mother's kiss being followed by her sleeping in his bed.

proceeded to Kazan and to Sergei in the hospital there, managing to make the long, precarious journey in a horse-drawn coach in an amazing forty-eight hours. On seeing her son, she again fell into a swoon that lasted nearly an hour.

It disturbed Sergei greatly that, when Maria Nicolaevna arrived, she insisted that he tell a lie and declare that he had pains in his knees—but the boy complied. The fear that Sergei was developing a "rheumatic condition," together with the intense reactions of mother and son, finally, after many weeks, convinced the school officials that the boy should go back home for another year in the country. At this point in his narrative, Aksakov writes about his "fits": "the hysterical seizures never returned" (47). This is most puzzling because later in that very book (1856b) he describes their recurrence.

Return to Mother

Sergei was ecstatic at the return. He had, interspersed with his illnesses, lived so happily, so blissfully at home, as the idol of his wet nurse and his mother. That rapture returned when he and his mother came back to Aksakovo for his year of respite from school. It began on the homeward journey. It was a beautiful morning in spring, and, in the carriage on the journey home,

> when I awoke, bright sunshine was pouring into the carriage. . . . My mother was sitting beside me, weeping tears of joy and gratitude to God; and her eyes showed her feeling so clearly that any spectator of her tears would have rejoiced and not grieved. She embraced her darling child, and a torrent of tender words and caresses shows what she was feel-

ing. It was the *19th of May, my sister's birthday. It was
a real May day; the spring morning* was warm, even
hot, and flooded all the landscape with burning
light. *The green fields of young corn, the meadows and
woods peeped in at the carriage windows;* I felt such
a desire to survey the whole wide prospect, that I
asked to have the carriage stopped. Then I sprang
out, and began to run and jump *like a playful child
of five,* while my mother watched me with delight
from the carriage.[20] For the first time, I felt I was
completely free. (57; emphasis added)

This was the full promise of spring—that delightful time for a
young boy and a young man, but the memory of that ecstatic
May subsequently would evoke the great sorrow of loss.

Aksakov writes about the end of the journey home: "I
shall not try to describe what I felt when I saw my dear Aksakovo. Human language has no words adequate to express
such feelings" (1856b, 60). This bliss shored up the boy's conviction that there was no life without mother.

Re-separation from Mother

The year of reprieve was spent in large part in passionate fishing and hunting—activities the boy had begun at Aksakova
when he was five. They had been vehemently disapproved of
by his mother. But Sergei at eight became obsessive with these
activities that he was able to share with great joy both with his
father and his body servant and companion, Yevséich (a ma-

---

[20] When he was five the boy was still involved with a symbiotic attachment to his mother; but that lessened as he started his intense interest in
fishing at eight.

ternal father figure). The boy's pleasure and his achievement of a reinforcement of his masculine identity at this time helped him make a partial transition from mother to Mother Nature. It was a great step in the direction of attaining a separate identity. In relation to the killing of fish, fowl, and animals, he could express some of his repressed rage toward his beloved but disapproving mother on whom he was still so emotionally dependent. The mother without whom he had heretofore felt he could not live became the mother he could *also* at least transiently live without.[21] This modification probably made going back to the school in Kazan tolerable for him.

Regression

But there was a regressive return of symptoms toward the end of the year when the time to leave his parents and go back to Kazan was approaching. He writes, "It is true that I had not a single seizure after leaving school . . . but now I became excessively restless and began to talk in my sleep every night. . . . I began also to cry and sob in my sleep, to jump out of bed and try to walk out of the room. *I slept with my parents in their bedroom, and my bed was close to theirs.*[22] My nocturnal distress grew worse every night" (67–68; emphasis added). He would also spring out of bed at times with a piercing cry and stare wildly around, repeating over and over again a disjointed and

---

[21] This is an example of "object constancy," a term that will be described and explained in the appendix.

[22] This was a position for experiences of, or at least fantasies about, seeing and hearing parental intercourse (primal scene). If so, these would have been frightening and colored by the view of his father, and now of himself, as killers of fish, birds, and animals and possessors of weapons—the stuff of sadomasochistic fantasies that contained both excitement and deadly dangers to all three participants in the primal scene of incestuous drama.

meaningless phrase, such as, "Let me go!"—"Go away"—"I can't"—"Where is he?"—"Where shall I go?" From these cries it sounds as if the boy felt he was being chased and attacked. He reports, "Sometimes I fancied vaguely that I had dreamt of something falling upon me and smothering me, or of monsters pursuing me" (69).[23] These cries and fancies were followed by his compulsively darting around the room. And then, Aksakov continues, "This kind of attack always ended with a severe fainting fit. The swoon passed into sleep. *My face was convulsed and I foamed at the mouth,* while unconscious" (69; emphasis added).

This certainly sounds like "hysterical seizures." They were perhaps unconsciously partly motivated to interfere with his parents' sexual coupling. He certainly interrupted his parents' sleep for hours by these fits that clearly made the boy and not the parents the center of attention. Mother had to attend to him rather than to father. "I remembered waking for some reason in the night, to find my parents and others standing by my bed" (69). Finally some sort of folk medicine, suggested by his aunt, brought the attacks to a halt.

Recovery After Separation

On his return to school in Kazan, the hysterical seizures never did recur, and Sergei was able to become a diligent and contented student throughout his subsequent teenage years. As his school years continued, Sergei's leaving for Kazan after the long holidays increasingly evoked a preponderance of anticipatory pleasure, accompanied by some regret rather than the dread of going back to school. "The second parting from my mother

---

[23] He seems here to be playing the role of the masochistic, passive victim, underneath the monster.

did not cost me anything like the pain and misery which had accompanied our former separation. I noticed the difference in myself especially, young as I was, I was impressed by it and had some regretful thoughts. . . . [but] by degrees I became accustomed to school-life, made some real friends among the boys, and became fond of the school" (96–97).

Sergei did very well scholastically and lived outside of school, mostly with teachers who were his tutors. At one point he was living in a sort of boardinghouse, and his good feelings about the ladies there who were kind to him made his mother jealous: "To my great astonishment, [mother] disapproved also of the notice taken of me by the kind ladies at my boarding house, and especially of the blandishments of one of [my tutor's] sisters [there]. She [again] decided to travel to Kazan in winter; she wished to see my manner of life for herself" (112–13). Maria Nicolaevna was basically upset because of Sergei's contentment at the school, away from her. He writes, "By this time I had become strongly attached to the school, the masters, and the boys, in whom I found cheerful companions" (113).

Kartashevsky

Sergei's mother was somewhat comforted when the boy shifted to, and lived with, her favorite tutor at the school, Kartashevsky, a reserved but brilliant teacher who had at first refused to take the boy on. Kartashevsky, who had finally been persuaded by Maria Nicolaevna to become Sergei's tutor after the first tutor was no longer available, subsequently traveled back to Aksakovo with Sergei for a long visit. (And, many years later, he married Aksakov's beloved younger sister.) Aksakov writes about him, "I felt a profound respect for him, and even loved him. . . . My life with Grigori Kartashevsky is one of the happiest memories of my early youth. It lasted two years and a half.[24] It was long before he consented to take me [as a special pupil], but once he consented, he devoted himself to me heart and soul. My school lessons, though I continued to do well with them, [became less important], and my private instructions [by Kartashevsky] became the main business" (119–21).

Kartashevsky brought a reinforcement of male influence by a confident and intellectual man very unlike Sergei's father. But evidence of a profound ambivalence for his mother's favorite tutor exists in the great difficulty the exceptionally intelligent youth (who was regarded by the whole school as a kind of prodigy) had with the subject of mathematics—which was Kartashevsky's special field.[25] This clearly seems neurotically based: "It is an odd fact that I was positively unable to learn mathematics. I cannot say that I did not understand [Kartashevsky's] uncommonly clear explanations, but I forgot instantly what I understood. In respect of mathematics, my excellent memory proved no better than a clean sheet of white paper, which refused to retain a single mathematical sign!" (120–21).

But for Sergei the residual resistance to the person one loves here was turned to an admired father figure (at least preponderantly) who could be stern and say no. The relationship with his tutor was able to help him separate from his mother psychologically, despite its probably having been partly based on Sergei's relationship to her. And he also developed a new closeness to his father when he was home on the long holidays from school. He would appear to have modified the intensity of the danger of separation from his mother and, in the rest of

[24] This was from Sergei's ages fifteen to seventeen.

[25] "I continued to work with [my tutor] at foreign languages, especially French, and in three months I could read it fluently and understand any French book. I had the memory of youth, and I was able to repeat next morning, without having learned them, the French original, my Russian translation and the separate list of words I had studied the night before" (121).

the book on his education, she appears mainly as a background figure. She is mentioned (1856b) as the one who disapproves of Aksakovo and the hunting and fishing Sergei so fervently pursued there with the backing and, usually, the participation of his father or of Yevséich.[26] Here is his reaction to catching his first really huge fish: "In my joy I shook *like a man* in a fever— indeed that often happened afterward when I caught a large fish; *for I could not calm down, but kept running constantly to look at* my prize, as it lay on a grassy bank a safe distance from the water. . . . This early success confirmed at once all *my passion* for fishing" (72–73; emphasis added). My italics here are meant to emphasize my speculation that in these masculine aggressive pursuits, here in relation to a "large" phallic object, the boy was reversing the passive and feminine masochistic position in the primal scene associated with his former separation symptoms, a remnant of which was (perhaps) his compulsively "running constantly to look at" the big fish. There is a transformation here, both from passive to active and from masochistic to sadistic. There is still anxiety with the excitement, so he shakes, but "like a man." The anxiety-ridden being pursued by a monster has now become Sergei's catching and killing the monster, the boy reversing roles to be himself a sort of monster in relation to his piscine, avian, and animal prey.[27] This being the aggressor is reinforced: "In the summer holidays three years later [when] I fired a gun for the first time, and my fate was fixed: all other sports, even fishing, lost their charm

---

[26] "My father and I listened with mortification to the eloquent invective she often aimed at Aksakovo, and though we did not defend it, our hearts were not convinced" (74).

[27] He also at this time became fond of hawking: "I had a little hawk of my own, very well trained, with which I caught sparrows and other small birds" (73). Also, "Another great occupation of mine was to lay traps for small animals—martens, ermine, and stoats. The soft pretty skins of my victims were hung up as trophies by my bed" (77).

in my eyes, and I became and remained throughout life a *passionate lover of the gun"* (73; emphasis added).

Aksakov writes about the year after he returned to school when he was fifteen, the year father promised him that during the next long vacation he would buy him his own gun: "The spring of 1804 came around. Spring disturbed my attention and reminded me too much of spring at Aksakovo, the budding sportsman could not hear with indifference the cries of the returning birds" (126). The promise of spring is now the promise of shooting his own gun. So the fifteen-year-old Sergei wants to go back home— but primarily to father, or at least to father's interests, rather than to mother. Subsequently, "my father kept his promise to me, he had got me a light gun. With my first shot I killed a crow, and that settled my fate. I went mad over shooting. The next day I shot a duck and two snipe, and my madness was confirmed. Fishing and hunting were forgotten; carried away by my excitability, I ran about with the gun all that day and dreamt of the gun at night. . . . I ate little and slept badly. I grew brown as a gypsy, lost flesh visibly; but I never stopped shooting" (133–34). I speculate that here he ran around and dreamed of killing rather than having the disturbing somnambulistic "running around" night symptoms of earlier years. This would imply that his murderous aggression had been externalized in a way that relieved his inner psychic conflicts. He was shooting and killing birds and animals, not his beloved mother, sister, or father. Still, he was disturbed enough to eat little and sleep badly. But the enhanced identifications with his father, Yevséich, and now his tutor went along with his continuing ability to do well both at home in the presence of, and at school away from, mother.

I feel that my speculations are confirmed by a passage later in the book about Aksakov when he was seventeen and attending college in Kazan: "I went to lectures at the college. I began a course on anatomy with much interest, and enjoyed the lecture, as long as the dissection was confined to animals, living or dead. But, when it came to the dissection of corpses, I gave up anatomy for good. I was afraid of dead bodies. . . . When the Bursar of the school died, I was much attached to him but I had been afraid from childhood of the sight of a dead body, and therefore in spite of the arguments and remonstrances of my tutor, I positively refused to attend the funeral" (164, 168). The relationship to the tutor Kartashevsky was an important transitional step. He was not mother but was associated with her because of her positive prejudice toward him. Kartashevsky was benevolent but strict, demanding, and emotionally distant. Sergei achieved a sense of a permissible distancing compatible with remaining emotionally attached to an ambivalently loved and needed person. Kartashevsky, like his mother, both set an example for and encouraged Sergei's avid interest in learning.

College

The teachers at the school in Kazan in 1804 reorganized the gymnasium (high school) and established a college in which Kartashevsky was a professor and Sergei continued his education. During his three years there (ages fifteen to seventeen) he became passionately interested in acting in the theatrical company the students formed, where he became the principal male lead and the manager of the troupe. His public performances were good enough to attract praise from a noted professional actor. The interest in the theater was also a sign of rebelling against his mother's wishes. She had disapproved of her son's attending the amateur performances at Aksakovo in his boyhood years.[28] The avid theatrical interest continued after Sergei received his leaving certificate from the college. Kartashevsky, in contrast to Maria Nicolaevna, approved of and shared this interest. A year or so before Sergei finished college, however, Kartashevsky became angry with him, largely in relation to the youth's refusing to attend the funeral of the school's bursar,[29] of whom Sergei had been fond, and the youth left his tutor's house. (But the two were reconciled in later life.)

Leaving School

About this time, his parents inherited much wealth from his father's aunt. Sergei was eighteen (this was 1808) when he left Kazan and Aksakovo behind to take a job in government service, first in St. Petersburg and then, three years later, in Moscow, in or near which he was to spend most of his future life. The war with Napoleon had begun two years previously, but the French invasion of Russia was still four years in the future (1812).

A Russian Schoolboy is as far as Aksakov went with his autobiography. His last volume of memories was about the life of his grandfather and his parents, and the rest of his life after college is not known in the marvelous detail he supplied in writing about himself.

Reversals of Feelings about Aksakovo

Just before leaving for St. Petersburg, Aksakov returned to Aksakovo: "Just before the snow melted in spring, [I went back] to Aksakovo and there I found spring and outdoor sports. Na-

[28] The theatricals there were the passion of his aunt, Maria Nicolaevna's former enemy; she would sneak the boy into the room where the performances took place, without the knowledge of his mother.
[29] Who probably unconsciously evoked for Sergei both his father and his tutor.

ture was awakening from her winter sleep, and the migrating birds were returning. *It was the first time I had really seen and really felt that season;* and the effect was to banish from my head for a time all thought either of the war with Napoleon or of the University and the companions I had left there" (193; emphasis added).[30] The statement I have italicized at first seems strange, given all his rapturous descriptions of spring. But perhaps Aksakov is paying tribute to his feeling grown-up and able to observe himself and his feeling of a separate identity with more tranquility.

Nessun Maggiore Dolore at Aksakovo

Sergei had long reversed his first painful, humiliating reaction to his visit to Aksakovo when he was five. The initial hatred of Aksakovo turned, in a characteristic way for Aksakov, to passionate attachment. There followed more reversals of feeling about the estate. Aksakovo became, once he started to live by himself and especially after his marriage,[31] a place to avoid living in when he could.[32]

In his memoirs, Aksakov followed the description of his great happiness at the return from Kazan with his mother for the year off after his "epilepsy" with the following passage: "I continued throughout my life to feel, when approaching Aksakovo, the same emotion as I did then. But some years ago I was getting near the place after an absence of twelve years. Again it was early morning; my heart beat fast with expecta-

---

[30] These are the final words of *A Russian Schoolboy.*

[31] Akakov lived for most of the rest of his life in or near Moscow. Most of his last years were spent on an estate he bought for his growing family about thirty miles outside of Moscow. He inherited Aksakovo after his father died.

[32] There were two periods of some years of his living there, in between civil service assignments.

tions, and I hoped to feel the happy excitement of former days. I called up the dear old times, and a swarm of memories came round me!" But this time what the middle-aged man felt was again clearly something like Dante's *dolore:* "Alas! They brought no happiness to my heart but only pain and suffering, and I felt heavy and sad beyond expression. Like the magician, who sought in vain to hide from the spirits he had called up but could not control, so I did not know how to banish my recollections and lay the storm of my troubled heart. Old bottles will not hold new wine, and old hearts are unfit to bear the feelings of youth. But *then*—ah, what were my feelings *then!*" (60–61).

In part because of this Dante-like mental anguish associated with Aksakovo, Aksakov could not bear to go back there from Moscow in the years after he had married and lived with his wife. His mother and father were living there. The young couple had lived with them at Aksakovo for a few years in between Aksakov's government assignments, and it had not been a happy time.

But an even more commanding reason for this avoidance of his old home as an adult was the estrangement from his mother, who openly and vigorously expressed resentment at his marriage. She could not accept it, and she turned, bitterly, against her best-beloved son. When his parents died, Aksakov inherited Aksakovo, which he would go to visit, but he continued to live in his estate near Moscow.

Later Life

After Sergei's marriage, Maria Nicolaevna became increasingly disturbed and difficult to live with, quarreling with her feckless and sometimes—she suspected, apparently with reason—unfaithful husband. Sergei's aversion to visiting Aksakovo continued even after her death. He was, I believe, subject to a life-long compulsive paradoxical repetition of not being able to bear the thought of living apart from his mother (at first consciously and then unconsciously) while desperately wanting (at first unconsciously and then consciously) to separate from her. There must have been a regressive return and reliving of his childhood and youth for the blind old man as he was writing his memoirs. It involved a revival of the childhood idealization of his now-dead mother (after the quarrels and bitterness with her of the later years). Yet in his writings a wonderful objectivity emerged. Perhaps this ability to transcend his emotional conflicts was abetted by another regressive revival of the earliest steps toward separation as he was writing his books on fishing and hunting at the same time that he was writing his autobiography. This could have reinforced his ability to maintain the separation from his mother at the same time he was reviving the attachment with her as he transcribed his childhood. (Of course separation from the parent in development always involves some identification with them—an unconscious taking of some [usually distorted] part of them as part of one's own identity. I have tried to point out some of these identifications.)[33]

Aksakov as Father—Konstantin

Sergei Aksakov was apparently close to all of his many children.[34] A specific identification with his mother and her early relationship with him was, however, strikingly repeated in Sergei's closeness to *his* talented firstborn son, Konstantin.

[33] Identifications with his grandfather are also to be noted.
[34] Fourteen children were born; nine of them survived past adolescence.

During his father's many years of increasing blindness, Konstantin was the one who read excerpts from his father's work in public. Konstantin was also a writer. He and his brother Ivan (another writer) became well-known leaders of the Russian Slavophile movement. Something was strange about Konstantin. He apparently was never able to achieve a social life apart from his family. He probably never had sexual relations with women or men. Durkin writes, "[The father's] relationship with his eldest son might well be termed excessive. Sergei Timofeevich had taken care of Konstantin in his infancy, behavior almost unheard of for men among the gentry at the time. In later years the two were virtually never apart.... Sergei Timofeevich's over-protectiveness with Konstantin rendered his son relatively helpless in practical matters, a situation he regretted but from which both father and son presumably benefited emotionally" (1983, 37; emphasis added). The last phrase seems naïve or ironic. Perhaps they may have in some ways felt the symbiotic closeness as a benefit, but one feels that for the son the cost was great. Sergei's repetition of his early relationship with his mother—surely an unconscious becoming his mother in relation to his beloved firstborn son—seems obvious. Konstantin, despite the accomplishments he had achieved with his writings, became as a young man no longer able to function independently and retired to the country. He subsequently even slept in the same room with his father. Sergei Timofeevich in 1844 wrote to his writer son Ivan of his worries about how disturbed Konstantin was acting, "his sickly condition is the heaviest stone upon my heart." (The "emotional benefit," if it ever existed, was no longer extant.) The despairing and guilt-ridden father expressed the feeling of being "convinced in my conscience that [I am] responsible." He adds, "The main thing is [Konstantin] can never be happy in life. Only within his family, surrounded by tender familial concern, can he exist and find some comfort. The world outside, to which he is not indifferent, will crush him. His successes, the highest public esteem of him . . . mean nothing" (quoted in Durkin 1983, 37). The father's psychological-mindedness is apparent here. He knew his son could not live without father.

Sofia

There developed, however, another intense but more happy and idealized relationship with Sergei's second son, Grigori, the first of his sons to marry, and especially with Grigori's wife, Sofia. In his fondness for this daughter-in-law, Sergei relived his grandfather Stepan's unexpected special favoritism toward Sergei's future mother, Maria, when she became the old man's daughter-in-law. It is surely significant that Sergei in his family memoirs replaces his mother's name, Maria, with Sofia's, retaining his mother's patronymic Nicolaevna; his heroine becomes Sofia Nicolaevna.[35] Durkin (1983) writes, "In some of his letters to [this] daughter-in-law, Sergei Timofeevich affects a folksy, old-fashioned style, not unlike that he later would assign to his . . . patriarch, Stepan Mikhailovich, in *Family Chronicle* [*A Russian Gentleman*]" (38).

In his adult years, so long after he had grown apart from his mother and even longer after the death of his paternal grandfather, Sergei was—in relation to his own children—still psychologically clinging to those important early ties by his (unconscious) repetitions of them.

---

[35] Durkin (1983) points this out but adds that it may simply be coincidence; so it may, but that possibility would not seem too convincing to those who believe in the unconscious mind.

Sergei was apparently a fond husband; his marriage when he was twenty-five to Olga Semenovka Zaplantina (for whom he defied his mother) lasted over forty years. He was rarely away from his wife, so there are not many extant letters, and her personality has not been, and now apparently cannot be, clearly grasped. Sergei Timofeevich's parents quarreled increasingly and tragically in their later years, especially after Sergei and his wife left the family estate to work in Moscow. Sergei's mother railed against her favorite son's marriage from the first appearance of Olga, and her aversion toward and jealousy of her daughter-in-law were augmented when it became obvious that her son was contented with his wife. Sergei's son Ivan writes of his grandmother, "The once brilliant, passionate Maria Nikolaevna turned into an old, sickly, suspicious, and jealous woman, tormented 'til the end of her days by the awareness of her husband's insignificance and at the same time by jealousy concerning him, for she felt that he merely feared her, but that she had lost his heart. . . . Both the old people felt that [my father] had left their way of life behind" (quoted in Durkin 1983, 42). Maria Nicolaevna became blind in the 1820s and died in 1833 (when Sergei was forty-two). The years of bitterness before, and much quarreling with his father after, her death contributed to his dislike of returning to Aksakovo in later years. Sergei felt that his father was, after Maria Nicolaevna had died, openly living with the woman she had been jealous of, and he resented it. He was an infrequent visitor. The decades of dislike of being there (a return to feelings he had had as a boy during the time before his grandfather's death) are not mentioned in the predominantly happy memories of Aksakovo that are emphasized in the family memoirs.

But, despite Sergei's residual conflict-ridden identifications with, and avoidance of, Maria Nicolaevna as the almost symbiotically close and caring parent, she was hardly forgotten by her favorite child. He visited her grave two years after her death, accompanied by his dependent son-companion, Konstantin. Durkin (1983) quotes a letter to his wife, Olga: "On Saturday at ten in the evening we arrived [and] went directly to Mother's grave. . . . It is not necessary and I am unable to describe to you, my dear, all the various emotions I underwent. . . . That night and even the following one I could not close my eyes" (44).

Leonard Woolf on Aksakov

Leonard Woolf in his autobiography mentions that when he was trying to teach himself Russian at age forty-five he started to read Sergei Aksakov's memoirs of his childhood. Aksakov became known to English readers when translations of his memoirs started to appear in the 1920s, a period when discerning literate English men and women were eager to read the great nineteenth-century Russian authors. By then, Constance Garnett's (and other) translations of Tolstoy, Dostoyevsky, and Turgenev were being avidly read by English intellectuals.

One passage about Aksakov's depressed feelings when sitting in his garden as a schoolboy evoked Woolf's memory of his own "cosmic unhappiness" in the family garden when he was a child of five: "Aksakov's descriptions of the garden and the raspberry canes recalled to me most vividly my *spider haunted* London garden and the despair which came upon me that September afternoon.[36] I felt that what I had experienced

---

[36] Both Woolf and Aksakov were "mother-haunted."

among the spiders and ivy he must have experienced half a
century before among the raspberries in Russia" (1960, 28; emphasis added).

I am going to excerpt some of the passages that I believe
Woolf was alluding to; they come from Aksakov's last book of
memoirs, *Years of Childhood* (1858). The book was first translated into English from the Russian in 1916, and Woolf recalled
it when he was thinking of or actually writing about his own
early life. What he remembered of his reaction to that earlier
reading must have led to the evocation of the physical setting
of Woolf's own childhood home garden and his terrifying experience there. Aksakov is describing the garden of his first
house in Ufa, when he was five and his sister three: "The two nurs-
eries in which I and my sister lived . . . were near my mother's
bedroom, and looked out into the garden; and the raspberries
planted below grew so tall that the canes peeped in at us through
the panes, which was a great comfort to me and my inseparable
companion, my little sister. The garden, though fairly large, *was
not pretty.* Here and there currant-bushes grew and gooseberries
and barberries and a score of *stunted* apple trees. There were
round flower-beds with marigolds, crocuses, and asters, but
not one large tree and *no shade. . . . Our poor town garden could
not satisfy me*" (1858, 9–10; emphasis added).

It was from the window that faced on this garden that
Aksakov as a child, when he was recovering from his early severe illness, admired the birds that led to his mother's gift of
the pigeons to which he became passionately attached. He also
wrote of that time of hearing a "strange, pitiful cry in the garden" (6). The boy had felt that someone was hurt, and his
mother sent a maid who brought in a recently born, still-blind
puppy. Feeling sorry for the puppy separated from his bitch
mother, the boy adopted him and trained him to lap up milk.

He became the mothering agent. The dog from the garden grew up to be a favorite yard dog of both son Sergei and mother Maria Nicolaevna.

Aksakov's Achievement

Aksakov is a wonderful writer and a great psychological observer. Many critics have praised his truthfulness and powers of description. Esther Salaman (1973) in her excellent book on autobiographies, writes that Aksakov's books about his childhood constitute a masterpiece of recollection that does not represent a translation of memories of experience into fiction: "I claim that [his] account of childhood [is] unsurpassed by . . . works of the imagination" (Salaman 1973, 3). Aksakov "does not invent: his impressions of people come best from himself . . . rather than from an omniscient narrator" (29). She quotes Tolstoy, who told a friend, "*The Years of Childhood of Bagrov's Grandson* is interesting because [Aksakov] himself describes his own impressions.[37] What is bad about novels is that description comes from the writer" (29).

Recapitulation

I want to underline the last part of the trajectory of Sergei's attachment to his mother that began at birth and continued for years as near-symbiosis, due to his illness and her overindulgence. This continued in a moderated way up to his school years in Kazan. The boy was initially separated from his father by this primary tie. As he grew older, however, his interest in

[37] In a diary entry of 1857, Tolstoy had called Aksakov's just-published book "ravishing" (Salaman 1973, 29).

his father increased, especially in relation to what became a shared passionate interest in the countryside, especially in hunting and fishing. (This tie to masculinity was reflected and abetted by the sharing of these interests with his body servant [and the guardian of his schoolboy years spent largely away from both parents], the serf Yefrem Yevséich.) Disagreement and hostility toward his mother for opposing the passion for blood sports, began to burgeon, and this fueled terrible intrapsychic conflicts for Sergei. There was increasing psychic separation dramatically enhanced by the physical separation that began in the years away at school (enhanced by the boy's relationship with his tutor). The separation culminated after Aksakov's move to Moscow and his marriage. There was a return, long after her death, to the old idealization of his mother when he began to work on his memoirs and recaptured the past. He was, soon after he started to devote most of his energies to his writing and publishing, unable to read and write for long periods of time and had to dictate his writings to others.[38]

Aksakov's relative objectivity about his grandparents and his parents did not prevent him from being haunted by them, by their imagos. We are all so haunted, but the intensity of the haunting exists over a wide spectrum. The pathology (symptoms and inhibitions and character distortions) is present alongside the benefits of the positive side of our psychic internalizations of our parents and the retention of our early reactions to them. It seems to me obvious that Sergei benefited greatly from the positive qualities of his mother: her intelligence, her intense caring, her interest in learning and books. The presence within our psyche of partly absorbed versions of these

----

[38] Aksakov really worked as a professional writer only in the last fifteen years of his life (from age fifty-three to sixty-eight).

once all-powerful parental identities can, alongside the damage to the child's separate identity, provide and enhance, like the dybbuk of Jewish mythology, great positive powers and even contribute to creative gifts.[39]

When the first fragments of his memoirs were combined and published as a book (1856a), Aksakov added the following moving statement as an epilogue:

> Farewell, my figures, bright or dark, my people, good or bad—I should rather say, figures that have their bright and dark sides, and people who have both virtues and vices. You were not great heroes, not imposing personalities; you trod your path on earth in silence and obscurity, and it is long, very long since you left it. But you were men and women, and your inward and outward life was not mere dull prose, but as interesting and instructive to us as we and our life in turn will be interesting and instructive to our descendants. You were actors in that mighty drama which mankind has played on this earth since time immemorial; you played your parts as conscientiously as others, and you deserve as well to be remembered. By the mighty power of the pen and of print, your descendants have now been made acquainted with you. They have greeted you with sympathy and recognized you as brothers, whenever and however you lived, and whatever

---

[39] The importance of the positive elements of even an almost symbiotic relationship to a parent (and its subsequent internalization) can also be seen in Sergei's talented son, Konstantin, before his pathological regression as an adult.

clothes you wore. May no harsh judgement and no
flippant tongue ever wrong your memory! (208)

It is an elegiac soliloquy commenting on human life and the
passage of time that ends the book in very much the same tone
of longing for the past that Anton Chekhov is to give his characters in his great full-length plays (in arias, duets, and trios)
fifty years later. The resignation and despair about the future
are more implicit in Aksakov. But both writers lived and wrote
with great wisdom and dignity about a life in which the
longed-for idealized parents can no longer figure. To use a
Chekhovian image, the family cherry orchard needs (alas!) to
be chopped down.

XI
On Listening, Knowing, and Owning

The human mind is not a dignified organ, and I do not see how we can exercise it sincerely except through eclecticism. And the only advice I would offer my fellow eclectics is: "Do not be proud of your inconsistency. It is a pity that we should be equipped like this. It is a pity that Man cannot be at the same time impressive and truthful."

—E. M. Forster, Aspects of the Novel

The English novelist E. M. Forster is here (1927, 147) expressing a typical two (not three) cheers for eclecticism—and distrust for the certain, the perfect, the absolute.[1] Yet we need to feel that we know what is occurring and what has occurred. It helps to know that there is a paradox about the ability to know.

Clinical Example

V, who complained of feeling haunted, came to see me years ago after reading my *Soul Murder* book because he was obsessed with the idea that he had been seduced as a child by his father. He made a valiant attempt at analysis but finally ran away from the treatment rather than allowing himself to gain any conviction, one way or another, about the actuality of having been abused. (The terror of his destructive rage at his father and, in transference, at me seemed to be too much for him to bear.) But there could be no doubt about the intensity of his listening in the *expectation* of being attacked. Any movement I made in the chair behind him, any change in my breathing pattern or in the emotional tone of my voice, was usually immediately noted and evoked intense anxiety. He would tell me that I was stifling a cough or yawning, and sometimes he was right in the frequent descriptions based on his hyperperceptiveness. This seemingly adaptive hyperawareness was matched by a need to block out things massively. (These contrary directions— to know and not to know—seemed to operate in two nonconnecting compartments of his mind.) He had for years little idea either of what I or the room beyond the couch looked like. He would repeatedly "discover" what he felt were new pieces of furniture, pictures, or ornaments in the room, most of which

[1] One of his essays is titled "Two Cheers for Democracy."

had been there from the beginning of his treatment. These discoveries were always announced in a tone of accusation.[2] I have found that many patients, particularly those who were abused as children, possess this coexistence of contradictory intense perception (listening, seeing, smelling) and intense blocking of perception and a sense of knowing.

Owning—A Clinical Example
(Dr. Harrison's Patient, B)

I will present a short clinical example that illustrates a step on the path to *owning* in a child. It is not from my own practice, but from a wonderful videotape made by Dr. Alexandra Harrison of a session with her patient B, a little girl of five. This perhaps five-minute fragment of a session seems to demonstrate the little girl's beginning to own her hostility toward her analyst. It is a beautiful demonstration of the back-and-forth flow of feelings between the two participants. One sees B's defensive turning away, followed by a turning back toward the analyst. One sees and hears her anxiety, her ambivalence, and her specific defensive need to change the subject—all culminating in demonstrating what appears to be a preliminary ability to accept and acknowledge through the mutual work. One realizes that much more repetition will be required, but B appears to be launched on the way to owning the coexistence of her hostile and positive feelings toward the new parental figure.[3]

I will not present anything of the case history except to say that little B, a very well-behaved child—probably too well-behaved—has just started treatment in large part because of the onset of terrifying nightmares. The analyst feels that the

---

[2] As if he were saying, "Look what you've done to me!"
[3] B seems to be a "natural"—a psychologically gifted little patient.

little girl is terrified of her rage.[4] In the videotape, Dr. A. (as I shall call her) and patient B are sitting on the floor playing with a toy village. The play is a continuation of what had begun in the previous session.

Session (A. = analyst; B. = patient)

Speech	Nonverbal Process
A. Oh, I know. They were going places they weren't supposed to go, and the policeman was telling them to get out.	
B. Yeah. This is one of the sisters. This is the big sister, right? And This is the little sister. Now we Need the firefighter.	Orients to A. Direct gaze
A Oh yeah, right.	
B. And you know what we also need?	Positioning figures behind her. A. goes into playroom
A. What?	
B. The doll case. The doll basket.	
A. Want me to get the firefighter?	Brings in the firefighter
B. Yep, they're in that building they are not supposed to be in!	Looking at toys, not at A. Sits up and moves toward A, gaze averted.
A. Uh-oh!	
B. Where is he?	
A. Here's the policeman.	She holds up police doll
B. He has a big smile on his face.	Takes and examines him
A. He does have a big smile.	Looking at doll

[4] As I have said, simply feeling intense rage that the child feels can kill can be traumatic for the child.

B. "*You* get outa here! *You* get outa here! *You* get outa here! *You* get outa here!"	repetitive invariant tone
[sisters say:] "No, we won't!"	slightly different tone
A. "No, we won't!"	
B. "No, we won't!"	puts dolls in building
A. "No, we won't! We *never* will get outa here!	
B. "No, we never will!"	moves dolls inside building

[Note how the intuitive therapist repeats and mirrors the words and, as the video shows, the movements and even the facial expressions of the child. Then, when the therapist (as one of the sisters) extends the dialogue—adding an observer to the characters, the little patient repeats and mirrors the therapist.]

A. What happened? Where did they go?
B. They're going *up* into the building.
A. Oh, gosh. Right. Where they're not supposed to be. They got away from the policeman and went right back to where they *wanted* to be and where he told them *not* to be!
B. "Hee, hee, hee," said the little sister!
A. "Hee, hee, hee," said the big sister too! "We can go anywhere we want! That dumb policeman can't tell us where to go, right, sister?"

B. No-o!	makes noise by cranking door of jail
"Hey! You get out there and go . . . to . . . jail!"	Looks up suddenly at A with anxious laugh.
"You have to be sep-a-rated in jail!"	Same cadence in both sentences.

A. The two sisters separated?

B. Yep!

A. Oh, no! They don't want that!

B. Well, they have to be sep-a-rated!

A. That's a terrible punishment for   Dismayed tone
   them!

B. And they don't have their Mom!   Face and body tense

A. They don't have their Mom?

B.   Nods head in exaggerated
                                             way, mouth in tight smile

A. "I want my Mom! Where's my   A's voice high-pitched
   Mom?"   doll's voice
   "I want my Mom!"   Direct gaze at A., still tight
                                             smile

B. "Hee, hee, hee!"   Very softly, looks up
                                             anxiously at A.

A. The policeman won't let them call
   their Mom? He just went "hee, hee,
   hee"?   B nods

A. Oh, no! That's really scary.   B turns to fire engine and
                                             examines it.

B. How does this [fire engine]
   get around?   A shows how the engine
                                             works

B. Oh. This is where fire people . . .   Puts fireman in chair of
   sit, right?   fire engine

A. Mm-hm.

B. There's only room for one fire-   Gets up and approaches
   person. Hey, maybe this other one   toy basket, crouches be-
   can be over here. Where is the other   side it
   fire person? Look for it.

A. Know what I think?

B. What?

A. I think the little girl being in jail
   without her Mom was so scary that

you started to play with the fire
engine instead. . . .
B. No.

[A.'s apparently premature connection is negated by B.]

A. No, you don't think so? That was
my idea.
Where is that other firefighter?
B. Hmm . . . I thought I remembered
where it was.
I thought I did, but I don't know.   Both are looking through
A's basket

He has to be in here.
A. Missing a firefighter, uh-oh!
B. What?
A. I didn't find him *any*where. What
if we can't *find* him? *Then* what
would we do?
B. Only have one fireman.
A. Yeah.
B. That's bad.
A. Oh, I wonder what's so bad about
that?
B. Because what if one fireman dies?
A. Oh, you really have a point there.
That would be really scary and sad!
There'd only be one fireman left!
B. No, what if the only fireman there
were there, died and there was a fire?
A. Oh, there wasn't another one to
take care of the children and put
out the fires! Oh, my gosh! You are
right! I wasn't even thinking right
about it until you reminded me!
That is such a scary thought!

[Here the video sound is unintelligible. The patient apparently
says that something is funny.]

A. Did you notice that sometimes
   funny things take your mind off
   scary things?
B. I didn't really notice it.
A. Oh. Well I thought it was a very
   scary thought, that if there was one
   fireman, and [pause] he died, then
   there would be no fireman to
   protect the children against the fires.
B. I think I want to play with the doll
   house.

[The therapist has apparently confronted B with something
scary enough to cause her to change the subject by asking to
start a different play scenario.]

B. The big dolls' house.
A. The big dolls' house?
B. Yes.
A. You know, what if I get the little
   dolls' house out, because the big
   dolls' house is pretty big, and we
   don't have much time? We only
   have about 5–10 minutes left. OK?
B. Well, I like the big dolls' house.
A. (unintelligible)
B. Oh.   Sympathetic tone
                                       picks up fire engine. It
                                       falls apart, and then B
                                       turns around again with
                                       back to camera, facing toy
                                       building, gazing at A.

A. Remember the little house, the little
   apartment we played with in the
   big building?
B.   leans over and cranks the
                                                jailhouse door open.

[pause]

A. But that was not what you had in
   mind, right? There's that old jail!
   Hmm. I wonder if that little Dr. A.
   belongs in that jail?
B.   looks at A. and grins.
                                                Direct gaze. Relaxed tone.

I believe that the grin, the direct gaze, the relaxed tone will turn
out to be, if all goes well, the beginning of B's owning her
threatening rage as part of her ambivalence toward her parents
(and now toward the analyst as well). It is intense rage (as she
focuses it on them) that gives rise to her terror of separation
from, and loss of, any of the valued three people upon whom
she feels so dependent.

Ambivalence Can Make Any Change Feel Like Loss

For the patients I am describing, it is not only their rage that
needs to be distanced and not owned. They also do not want
to feel responsible for the incestuous sexual excitement and
the anxiety that also accompany and result from dependency
on the parents. The resistance of the "change means loss" patients becomes evident (as I have tried to exemplify) through
an insistence on interminable contact with the analyst, while
concomitantly wanting to get rid of him—or by actually leav-

ing the analysis as the threat of losing or even loosening the internal bonds to parents becomes too great to bear. They cannot own this aspect of their pathology.

Another Clinical Example of Owning: Patient W

A middle-aged woman, W, late in her analysis, had begun to develop intense and erotic transference feelings toward me— these and her concomitant sexual fantasies bothered her greatly. W was still in what she characterized as a bad marriage she had once considered good or at least good enough, even though either she or her husband had almost from the beginning threatened one another with separation. There had actually been one trial separation, but it did not last long. They subsequently settled for separate bedrooms in a kind of mock compromise. The bad marriage tie appeared to be strong and had continued for decades. Their mutual quarreling seemed to me to have made as close an emotional bond between them, perhaps even a closer one, than did the comparative peace of their good enough times. W's husband was a successful businessman, and she also had had a work background that made her knowledgeable about the world of business. She still took an occasional active role in his corporation affairs but had not worked steadily after the birth of their children.

Money was the central focus of their arguments. W's husband had always enjoyed gambling, but gradually he became almost addicted to it. With the increasing compulsion, he was turning into a fairly consistent and heavy loser. This had made for many transient financial crises that resulted in their having to give up vacations and to sell furniture and works of art that W did not want to give up. His business was lucrative enough to allow him to recover from the financial losses. It was his repetitive losses of control and unkept promises to reform that made her feel "like a helpless and furious child." He kept breaking his pledges to stop the gambling, becoming evasive and hateful when she reproached him. The tension over the hopeless repetitiousness of the pattern led to the decline of the marriage. Both husband and wife seemed essentially to deny and pretend away from their difficulties. Just before she entered analysis, W's husband had demanded that she sell some of her favorite jewelry (inherited from her grandmother), and she had, uncharacteristically, refused. W sought out psychiatric treatment because she realized she felt unable either to leave him or to stay with him.

W claimed her children had not been aware of the quarrels and crises in the household. There had always been enough money to get by, so their going to college had not been interrupted; they had not suffered real deprivation, but the danger of their doing so had intermittently been present. The children had grown up and were now independent. That had eliminated the validity of the couple's excuse that they were remaining together "for the children." Yet the marriage had not broken apart. They stopped having sex. Neither sought out lovers, and they kept going out together socially "to keep up appearances." W seemed enmeshed in lies and pretences. She wanted to get rid of her husband yet was unable to do so. This emotional double bind in W's marriage was currently being repeated in her analysis.

W's Past

Both of these "traps" experienced in W's adult life were replications of the rage, longing, and helplessness that resulted from the powerfully deep ambivalence toward both parents in

W's childhood. Her mother had been cold and hostile; her father didn't protect her and had a chronic illness that made for many situations in which he was not expected to survive. In relation to her analyst, W felt especially distressed and angry about the feelings of dependency and longing that accompanied her sexual wishes; she suppressed the rage of her frustration. W had for years in treatment manifested a stubborn resistance to owning the emotions that her intellect told her were there. Whenever the feelings were acknowledged, she would follow what appeared to be an admission with what might be called a disowning disavowal like, "But I already know that, I've known it all along" alternating with "I'm certainly not aware of feeling it." She had the capacity to know it "all along" intellectually but obviously did not feel the forbidden emotions, or at least not their potential intensity.

Dreams

Finally, a time came, after years of this kind of repetitive, stubborn resistance, of a change and attenuation of her disavowals— this change was first evident in relation to changes in her dreams, which started to become more frequent, more memorable, and more emotional. Of course at first W would dismiss the changes as being "only in my dreams," but it clearly was a change. Over a period of several months her dreams became more and more vivid, dramatic, and full of angry confrontations. I began to appear in them, usually as an untrustworthy or untruthful figure. After a long period of work on her dreams, she gradually became able to retain an increasing residue of responsible feeling about them. The dreams also began featuring the disappearance of her husband or his complete absence. And people began to die and be killed in them.

An Unusual Dream

Again, the dream I am about to report took place after I had announced the dates of my long August vacation. It did not, however, feature a garden. The dream had an unusual visual structure, and she also described it as being "different in many ways." The most striking aspect, to W, was how real the dream felt. "That has never happened before," she declared. "My dream was like a play in two loosely connected acts, yet it felt so real. I felt really there. In the first part I was very upset and angry, you and my husband were there and I was yelling at you. I've never had a dream before that was so lifelike. In the next part you and my husband were present too. It was in a hotel lobby. I told him he had to go, that this time I wanted a divorce. You just stood by. He then disappeared. Suddenly I was alone, you were not there, I felt good and free. When I woke at first I wasn't sure it was a dream or if it had really happened." This dream had a theatrical setting that seemed to me was expressive of the dramatic quarreling and threatening of the past, but the new factor was the contradictory feeling of reality and of real emotional force that W stressed as she was describing it.[5] It came as a kind of epiphany experience and marked a turning point in the analysis toward owning her rage and her wish to get rid of her parents, her analyst, and her husband.[6] A long period of working on this followed. What started in dream-consciousness became owned and available in waking consciousness. The marriage was still intact when she left, but

[5] Later in my practice I had a male patient who had a similar "strikingly real" dream that he awoke from not knowing if it had actually occurred that also marked a significant advance toward owning.

[6] "In Dreams Begin Responsibility," title of a poem by W. B. Yeats (1914).

luckily the changes in her appeared to have enabled both husband and wife to resume sexual relations. She said, somewhat hesitantly, "It has again become a 'good enough' marriage." I have not heard from her since she terminated treatment and do not know if this compromised but perhaps relatively happy ending, which now seemed to feature a different and better balance of knowing and not knowing (with increased owning), was maintained.

XII

Gardens, Unweeded Gardens, and the Garden of Eden— Death and Transience

O, that this too too solid flesh would melt,
Thaw and resolve itself into a dew!
Or that the Everlasting had not fix'd
His canon 'gainst self-slaughter. O God! God!
How weary, stale, flat, and unprofitable,
Seem to me all the uses of this world!
Fie on't, oh fie, fie! 'Tis an unweeded garden,
That grows to seed
—Hamlet, *I,ii,129–36 (emphasis added)*

In this soliloquy, Hamlet, in mourning for his father, disgusted with his mother's marriage with his uncle, is full of mostly hostile ambivalence and of conflict that involves guilt over parricidal and incestuous wishes. In his suicidal mood, he uses the "unweeded garden" image as symbol of "this world" and its corruption, of Denmark ("something is rotten in . . ." *Hamlet,* I,iv,90), of his incestuous mother and uncle, and of himself: body ("too too solid flesh") and mind.[1] Both the outer and the inner worlds are bad, dirty, anal (compare the unweeded garden of Leonard Woolf's childhood memories).

Garden as a Symbol

A garden as a place, and specifically as a place where things grow, can be a symbol in both the ordinary linguistic and in the Freudian sense (Shengold 1995, 197–201) of the body and of the womb. The "unweeded" modification makes it bad, infested, and dirty. This degraded, anal garden image is the contradictory dark side in contrast to the idealized, paradisial connotations of the Garden of Eden. Hamlet's garden here is the Garden of Eden *after the Fall,* and so after acquiring the knowledge of good and evil.

History

Evidence of gardens appears wherever there was enough civilization to leave pictorial or written records. Probably the first records are from Persia about 6000 BC, where the idea of the garden as paradise originated. This would fit with the traditional notion that the Garden of Eden had been located in

---

[1] "Solid" can connote erection. An alternative reading of the work in the manuscript has been "sullied": dirty, anal, corrupted.

Mesopotamia. The Middle Eastern conception of Paradise being a garden also appears in Mohammedan culture, where it is probably derived from the Old Testament. (The idea of paradise is in the Koran.) The earliest artistic visual depictions of gardens are in relief carvings of about 3000 BC from Egypt, which has a long history of gardening.

Enclosed Gardens

Evidence of gardens in ancient Greece dates from the fourth century BC. They are mentioned in Homer's *Odyssey*. Ancient Rome saw gardening become a widespread art, and there are pictorial records from the second century BC. They include pictures of enclosed gardens. Medieval gardens were frequently enclosed and tended to be in a courtyard of a building or in the cloister of a church, monastery, or convent. The first pictures of these date from about 1400. Many illustrations in medieval manuscripts present the Garden of Eden as an enclosed garden.

The Garden of Eden and Its Dangers

In Genesis, the Lord God creates heaven and earth from the void, next creates Adam, and then: "The Lord God planted a garden in Eden, in the east; and placed there the man whom He had formed. . . . The Lord God took the man and put him in the garden of Eden to till it and tend it. The Lord God commanded the man, saying, 'Of every tree of the garden you are free to eat. But as for the tree of knowledge of good and bad you must not eat of it. For as soon as you eat of it, you shall be doomed to die'" (Genesis 2: 8, 15–17). Here is the Old Testament myth of a paradise that can be seen as a metaphor of development beyond birth and earliest infancy as the beginning, and the beginning of the danger, as it appears in the primal garden.

That danger is, *above all, of knowing*. Death must not be known, sex must not be known, good and evil must not be known.

Next, God creates the beasts and makes Eve from Adam's rib: "The two of them were naked, the man and his wife, yet they felt no shame" (Genesis 3: 25). The serpent urges Eve to eat of the forbidden fruit. It implies that God is lying and tempts Eve with false promise: "You are not going to die. No, God knows that, as soon as you eat of it, your eyes will be opened and you will be the same as God in telling good from bad" (Genesis 3: 4, 5).

They eat of the fruit: "Then the eyes of both of them were opened and they perceived that they were naked" (Genesis 3: 7).

So, in the Garden, according to the Creation myth, begin shame, sin, guilt, and evil. The sin of eating the fruit involves competition with the parent/creator/God and his creations in relation to *knowing* as much as the primal parent. (This includes sexual knowing.) The path is now open to incest and murder. The promise of knowledge and power has led to sex and life as well as to separation, loss, and death. From the time of the Fall from grace and the expulsion from the Garden of Eden, the story implies, Death as well as life will inhabit Earth's gardens.

With the expulsion, life ceases to be eternal and becomes transient. And the short span of spring and of the flowers in the garden makes us aware of our own transience.

Transience

Freud (1916) writes in "On Transience," "The proneness to decay of all that is beautiful and perfect can, as we know, give rise to two different impulses in the mind. The one leads to aching despondency . . . while the other leads to rebellion against the fact asserted. No! It is impossible that all this loveliness of Nature and Art, of the world of our sensations and of the world outside, will really fade away into nothing" (305).

Spring and summer inevitably become winter. We all know, and poets and philosophers keep telling us, about the transience of our individual lives, of all life on the planet, of the existence of the universe itself. Such knowledge is painful and threatening, although it can supply us with a sense of the dearness of life, of the preciousness of being able to love others and ourselves, and art, music, mathematics, science, and of simpler interests, accomplishments, and the pleasures of being alive.[2] Freud (1916) writes, "I dispute the . . . view that the transience of what is beautiful involves any loss in its worth. On the contrary, an increase! Transience value is scarcity value in time. Limitation in the possibility of an enjoyment raises the value of the enjoyment" (305). Freud (like Pascal), with his essentially tragic view of life, was well aware that we still need to distract ourselves from our mortality and consequent sense of transience for most of the time.

The Transience of Loving

Another truth, easily known but rarely owned, is how changeable, at best, are our deepest loving feelings. There is so much ebb and flow in our knowledge about who we are and how much or little (as well as how) we feel—about ourselves, about others, about ideas and causes.[3] I was once present at a lecture

[2] An epitaph from "The Greek Anthology":

Stranger, greet Diogenes, buried beneath the earth, and pass on.
Go wherever you wish, and good luck attend you.
Struck down in my nineteenth year, I rest here in darkness—
But, ah, the bright sun! (Anonymous)

3. These emotional shifts can be viewed as fluctuations of owning.

by the Israeli novelist Amos Oz, who said, movingly, in response to a question from the audience about what was alleged to be the relative absence in his novel of loving relationships between men and women, "You know, for human beings, it is very, very difficult to love." Even in those who consider themselves, and who are, deeply loving, it is painful to realize how transient and variable is the ability to care about others, and sometimes even about oneself. So much of our waking life is spent in narcissistic concern and withdrawal. How easily and quickly we regress to, and then, hopefully, come back from, earlier stages of psychic development, becoming children or even infants again in relation to the capacity to care about others. And yet, although these generalizations hold, all of these kaleidoscopic and sometimes chaotic changes vary in range and rhythm and pattern in a unique way for each one of us. It is part of the job of the psychoanalyst to make these shifts clear to the patient, not by giving a philosophic disquisition, but in the course of describing and demonstrating the patient's patterns of emotional change (quick, slow, reluctant, flexible, etc.) and encouraging the exploration of the details and effects of such patterns. Awareness of the fragile transience of love (*caritas*)[4] serves to, as Freud suggests, make it all the more precious.

---

[4] Love in the sense of feeling the dearness of another human being.

XIII

"THE PROMISE" and Ibsen's *A Doll's House* and *Hedda Gabler*

What wondrous life is this I lead!
Ripe apples drop about my head;
The luscious clusters of the vine
Upon my mouth do crush their wine;
The nectarine, and curious peach,
Into my hands themselves do reach;
Stumbling on melons, as I pass,
Ensnared with flowers, I fall on grass.
Such was that happy Garden-state,

While man there walked without a mate:
After a place so pure, and sweet,
What other help could yet be meet!

But 'twas beyond a mortal's share
To wander solitary there:
Two paradises 'twere in one
To live in Paradise alone.[1]
—*from Andrew Marvell,* The Garden *(1681)*

Mysteries obscure the earliest time of psychic development—of human initial and subsequent early narcissism. Some generalities about beginning development and maturation can be firmly believed in, but details are not, and perhaps can never be, known with certainty. Observers of infant behavior do the (often impressive) best they can; with older children and adults one can try to reconstruct the actualities of the first years of life and, speculatively, to construct theoretical formulations. Narcissism is a multifaceted and dynamic collection of phenomena. I feel we can know, with conviction, that each person has an individual variety of these. One important cluster of narcissistic phenomena centers on narcissistic promise and entitlement.

[1] Joseph Summers (1961) asks whether this ambiguous poem might mean "a serious commitment to the retired life of contemplation in nature, or, by exaggerating its claims for the perfect and simultaneous ecstasies of the body, mind and soul in a world without women or effort" (14). (Is he trying to show a retired life to be pleasant or to be dangerous?) I feel that the misogynistic stanzas I have quoted also demonstrate the narcissistic promise of life in the Garden of Eden—only Adam and his Creator (a paradise of two—of parent and child), before Eve and before the Fall. (And there are other possible interpretations.)

The primal parent is the experiential prototype of the Creator from the first verses of Genesis. To be alone in the Garden of Eden, protected by God, who has created us—in a universe of two—and promised us dominion over every living thing, is a metaphor for our earliest sense of the centrality of self shared with the mother as our godlike primal parent. The child's nascent sense of identity involves a feeling of certainty that (when emerging from symbiosis) it will be cared for and favored by an all-powerful benevolent parental being. This is one meaning of Marvell's poem.

Narcissistic Promise

Some patients feel especially entitled to having all their wishes fulfilled and all their troubles taken away. We all retain some degree of this infantile narcissistic expectation that is latently present in all of us.[2] We all, as inferred from child observations and from later manifestations, feel our beginning awareness of being alive as being *everything*—and, after the primal parent starts to be registered as a separate person, deserving *everything*. Such promise is part of early narcissistic development. Everything will be provided by an omnipotent Other; life is to be lived in a universe of two. A confident prospect of transcendent transformation can be consciously and even blatantly manifest both in children, and—by way of fixation and regression—in childish, narcissistic adults, trying to live like Adam before the eating of the forbidden fruit and the loss of Paradise. For some, there may be a strong inborn tendency toward this aspect of narcissism. Marked insistence on narcissistic privilege can also

---

[2] There are myriad variations of the intensity, quality, and extent of narcissistic character.

exist in adults who have had to use some developmentally early form of denial or nonacceptance of maturation and of frustration to defend against intense or prolonged traumatic anxiety as children: overwhelming anxiety due to actually experienced deprivation or abuse,[3] or to some inborn deficiency, or to a combination of both.[4] Some almighty person (mother, father, a parental equivalent, or God) will restore one to the lost Eden of the womb.[5] Such promising expectations do not make for happiness. The present is experienced as frustrating and emotionally empty of promise. As we emerge from symbiosis, the promise of being restored to lost bliss is expected (consciously or unconsciously) to be fulfilled *tomorrow*, if not today. The loss of the sense of transcendent promise can be terrifying; therefore people who hold onto it without much modification wait passively (like little children) for rescue from without. They are averse to trying for changes that can result in maturation. But waiting passively for the promises to be fulfilled by others gives no mastery of external reality. Mastery is achieved only if changes, especially inner changes, are allowed and actively sought. Optimally, deficiencies and blocking of maturation are transient and reversible as reliance on others increasingly shrinks. But passive waiting for rescue can again be mobilized in anyone whenever an anxiety-provoking regression of func-

[3] What I have called soul murder can set in for adults when overwhelming trauma induces regression or in concentration camp experiences (in life). This is illustrated (in fiction) by the rat torture that overwhelms Winston Smith, and he looks forward to a future of "loving Big Brother" in Orwell's *1984* (1948).

[4] The omnipotent abusing or depriving figure will be transferred onto others (most significantly onto the mother and then the father during the oedipal period) and of course onto the analyst.

[5] For soul murder victims, an example of such a parental equivalent is (again) "Big Brother" in Orwell's *1984* (1948).

tioning occurs. Without sufficient inner maturational change
there remains a pathologically intense near-delusion that change
and power can come only from submission to, alternating with
compulsive defiance (= negative compliance) of, parental figures. For those whose psyche is haunted by parents, activity
aimed at change comes too often in the form of identifying
with the parental aggressor—another way of holding on to the
parental ghost.

Clinical Example: Patient E

One of my patients, E (at first with some humor but subsequently with increasing bitterness), called her vague but
insistent—indeed almost delusional—expectation of a miraculous transformation by an external rescuer "THE PROMISE"
(pronounced, as it were, in capital letters, in a tone of awe).
THE PROMISE had been made and brought into being by her
godlike father.

E, an attractive, intelligent woman in her late twenties, came to see me many years ago because of anxiety and
depression. She complained of an almost constant feeling of
dissatisfaction. E was unhappily married. She had done well
academically and had advanced quickly toward success in her
profession, yet was continually discontent with the work she
did and how she was regarded in the small but prestigious firm
where she was employed. She felt, bitterly, that others were
preferred to her. E suffered from what I have called malignant
envy[6] (see Shengold, 1995): the feeling that what others—even

---

[6] I will give an example of ordinary envy to contrast it with malignant
envy. A middle-aged but still attractive actress had, during a rehearsal period, begun an affair with a much younger male actor. The director, a bisexual man well known for brief sexual contacts with young members of his

if they were in other firms or in other fields—were given or had achieved had been taken away from her. Her overbearing father had seriously suggested that she would grow up to become the first American woman president. Such high expectations were taken in and registered in E's mind as THE PROMISE. The bright little girl had both welcomed and was frightened by the anticipation of such magical predictions. She could be brilliant in school, but there had been rare lapses into near failure when she felt teachers (especially male teachers) did not like her. When she was a small child, her parents had insisted on E taking an intelligence test. They expected she would be found to be a genius. But E did badly; she was pronounced to be of average intelligence. Her parents never mentioned the test again. E felt humiliated by the mediocre evaluation and was mortified by her parents' treating the intelligence test as if it had never happened.[7] She then resolved to, and succeeded in, outdistancing her classmates in grade school, high school, and college. Her parents continued to express their high expectations.

Both parents alternated between fulfilling E's every wish (when she was a child the family was very rich but subsequently lost its wealth) and insisting on her carrying out their goals (mostly set by her father). She had temper tantrums as a

---

casts, seemed to be showing sexual interest in her young lover. The director was an old friend. She, knowing her man, decided to tell him about the affair. The director responded with characteristic kindness and empathy. He said, "You know, my dear, when we go to bed at night, we all need someone to cuddle with." He then turned his attention to another member of the cast. He may have felt envy of the actress, but it was not malignant envy. To repeat, malignant envy involves feeling rage based on the delusional conviction (not always conscious) that what the envied one has or is has been taken away from oneself.

[7] E went on to adopt the parental defense of dealing with what occurred when it was unwelcome as (to use Freud's term) "*non arrivé.*"

child, but later these were suppressed. She became a good girl in relation to her father but was hostile and competitive toward her mother. (E had felt more intelligent and more attractive than her mother.) E was an only child, and her intense sibling rivalry (so often felt by only children) was evoked when dealing with her peers and competitors. She had a special animus against men and chose boyfriends that were initially idealized and would go on to reject them as defective: weak or shallow or needy. (She felt soon after her marriage that her husband, from whom she had expected so much, was all of these.)[8] E continued to achieve in her profession, although occasionally getting into (sometimes spectacular) trouble. She repeatedly survived the crises, feeling strengthened by the firm confidence that her father could and would always be there to rescue her from any danger—hadn't he always done so?[9] Even after she became skilled at rescuing herself, she was threatened by any long separation from her father. (E had always had a fear of flying; this inhibited her professional functioning.) She usually suppressed her anxieties and her bad expectations that existed alongside and were disguised by THE PROMISE. She had "that confidence of success that often induces real success" noted by Freud (1917, 156).[10]

I have mentioned E's THE PROMISE many times in interpretations to others of their defensive use of the feeling of narcissistic entitlement for the purpose of denying what made

---

[8] E's marriage in this respect resembled that of Ibsen's Hedda Gabler to George Tesman (see below).

[9] He had once saved her from drowning when she was swimming and a sudden storm arose.

[10] In relation to E, I would revise Freud's well-known quotation about men in relation to mothers to "A [woman] who has been the indisputable favorite of [her father] keeps for life the feeling of a conqueror, that confidence of success that often induces real success" (1917, 156).

them anxious. The fantasy that magical rescue will *certainly* be forthcoming is latently present in all of us—but in different intensities accompanied by varying degrees of credibility. The young child feels that parents have *promised* to guarantee the continuation of initial feelings of immortality, omniscience, and omnipotence. Burgeoning of feelings of entitled promise can ensue as defensive compensation for some combination of parental overindulgence; inability to say no; cruelty; sexual abuse; incapacity for loving; neglect. I will provide one minor example of E's exaggerated sense of promise.

E was both intelligent and efficient. She had attained a position as the head of a department in a well-funded organization that operated in a special, narrow professional research field. She was well paid. Shortly before she started in analysis, she had begun to provoke and quarrel with her superiors at work and now felt that her position might be in danger. She had no anxiety about this; another job could *certainly* be found. (THE PROMISE was evident here.) But when she started to explore the possibilities in her special field, E discovered that few positions were available; and at some places with vacancies there seemed to be a prejudice against women. E began to become uneasy. She needed her high salary to support her and her husband's lifestyle. Both of them were beginning psychoanalysis. E dominated her initially idealized husband, whom she now regarded as an idle ne'er-do-well, not able or not willing to earn much money. (They subsequently divorced.)

After a time during which E experienced short bursts of anxiety, she heard about a position in a firm in a nearby suburban town. When an official sounded very enthusiastic over the phone, she at once felt *certain* that her problems were over. *Of course* they would want her; *of course* they would be happy to pay her what she needed. E began to become even more provocative with, and more openly scornful of, her male chief executive. Her confidence seemed unrealistic. I pointed out that she appeared to be certain she would get and be content with the possible new job—despite not yet knowing what the people and the quality of the functioning at the new research center were like, what her salary would be, or even if she would get a job offer. She agreed but went on to treat my intervention as if it had not been said.[11] Sanguine certainty continued. THE PROMISE had attained an almost delusional intensity. The subsequent interview about the potential position quickly dissolved the quasi-delusion, but not before E's provocation had ensured that she could not keep the job she had. I felt that a large part of her motivation in enacting this self-defeating scenario was the wish to be unable to afford coming to an analysis that was threatening her psychic maintenance of THE PROMISE.[12] But she was fairly quickly able to get another job and to continue her analysis and her psychically internalized parental promise.

When, later on, her father died, she had not been able to accept (except intellectually) that he was gone and could now never fulfill THE PROMISE. I will return to E's story after supplying a contrasting literary example.

Ibsen's Nora in *A Doll's House*

I will illustrate the quasi-delusion[13] of THE PROMISE by presenting a précis (with comments) of Ibsen's prophetic[14] and profound play *A Doll's House* (1879).

The drama's protagonist, Nora Helmer, is a young mar-

---

[11] Another use of the defense of "*non arrivé.*"

[12] E had never really mourned her father; she had not been able to accept that he was dead and that his "Promise" could now never be fulfilled.

[13] See Shengold (1993), *Delusions of Everyday Life.*

[14] Ibsen was a great and early believer in the rights of women.

ried woman with three small children. Her husband, Torvald, a lawyer, has just been appointed the manager of a bank. Nora's mother died soon after she was born, and she has been brought up by her father, now also dead, and an old nurse who is still with her and in charge of raising the Helmers' three young children. Nora's father had regarded her as a plaything: an indulged pet or living toy who existed to amuse him. Nora's husband also exhibits the sanctimonious paternalism taken for granted by so many late nineteenth-century men. He is delighted with his pretty wife. He generally treats her kindly but does not take her seriously as a separate person—she exists to amuse and serve *him*. He is sexually enthralled by her but regards her as a fulfiller of his needs. That Torvald sees Nora as his possession is illustrated by a scene in act 3 in which the two come home from a party at which Nora had been enthusiastically applauded for dancing a tarantella. He is sexually excited, and Nora reacts negatively:

NORA. Don't look at me that way, Torvald.
TORVALD. I am not to look at *my* darling treasure?—
     at the loveliness that is *mine, mine* only, wholly
     and entirely *mine!* (1879b, 673; emphasis added).[15]

Torvald, continuing his wife's father's role toward Nora, regards her, the mother of his children, as a child to be indulged, played with, regulated (she is not allowed to eat macaroons), and occasionally scolded for her naiveté and extravagances. Torvald met Nora when he, a lawyer employed by the government, was

[15] "*Nora.* When we were first married [Torvald] was almost jealous if I even mentioned one of the people at home [in the North]; so I naturally gave up doing so" (660).

sent north to investigate her father, who had been charged with dishonesty. We learn later in the play that Helmer, the government investigator, was led to dismiss the allegations (which included a charge of forgery) against Nora's father because he had fallen in love with the accused man's daughter. Torvald had been selfish and dishonest. He had, in his action, put aside his righteous, strict standards of morality.

At the start of the play, Nora appears unaware that she is trapped in a doll's house. Both she and the house are, according to law, the property of her husband. Torvald is constantly, if affectionately, belittling his wife, calling her his little bird, his little sparrow, his little lark, his little squirrel.[16]

Nora has a guilty, terrible, but potentially wonderful secret—wonderful because she believes that in the dreaded eventuality of its being revealed, Torvald would see not only how deeply she has loved him, but also how much (beneath her carefree, merry doll façade) she has been a caring and responsible wife. One could call this belief her faith in THE PROMISE.

Torvald had become ill shortly after the couple married. His doctors told Nora that he would die unless he left Norway to recuperate in the sun of southern Europe. They lacked the money to go to Italy. Nora, without telling her husband, had borrowed it and, in doing so, had forged her dying father's name as guarantor of the loan. When Torvald recovered in Italy, they returned to Oslo.

Over the years Nora, slowly and without Torvald's knowledge, has been paying back the loan and interest to Krogstad, a

---

[16]This condescension was poignantly effective in the recent marvelous performance (in New York City and London) by the very tall Janet McTeer. That performance also stressed the sexual nature of the couple's relationship—and featured a more sympathetically portrayed Torvald (who so often has been presented as a one-dimensional tyrant).

former friend of Torvald's who, after disgracing himself as a lawyer, had become a usurer. Despite giving the impression of extravagance, Nora has been economizing by spending very little on herself and has managed to pay interest, using her own pocket money and not the money given her for household expenses. She has wheedled additional sums from her husband for purchases. She also has secretly been staying up at night doing copying work to earn money. She has done her confused best to keep up interest payments and pay back her debt to the usurer.

Christine, an impoverished, recently widowed childhood friend of Nora's, has just come south to Oslo to get a job. Christine remarks, after Nora has thoughtlessly described how carefree and happy she has been as Torvald's wife, that "[You are] a mere child . . . who know[s] little of the troubles of life." Nora reproaches her friend for being patronizing:

> NORA. You're like the rest. You all think I'm fit for nothing really serious. . . . I haven't told you *the great thing!* (1879b, 648; emphasis added)

Nora says that she also has sacrificed and worked hard and tells her friend about the debt (although not how it was obtained or from whom she had borrowed it):

> NORA. Yes—I too have something to be proud and glad of. I saved Torvald's life. (1879b, 648)

Torvald and everyone else believe that her father gave her the money, but she found a way to borrow it without Torvald's knowledge. Torvald, she explains, has "such a loathing of debt" (1879b, 649).

The usurer Krogstad, before the loan, had himself been

caught in an act of dishonesty involving forgery. He was able to escape jail ("by a trick," Torvald says) but has lost his position in society and his status as a lawyer. He has since been given a chance to redeem himself working as a clerk at the bank to which Torvald has just been appointed manager. Krogstad wants to give up his usury and, for the sake of his children (his wife has died), live a life of honesty. The pharisaical Torvald is determined to dismiss Krogstad, whom he despises as dishonest. Torvald finds it intolerable that the clerk (presuming on their boyhood friendship) treats him, his manager, with familiarity.

Krogstad comes to the Helmer home and tells Nora he knows she forged her father's name as guarantor on the loan document. Nora, in Oslo, had unknowingly dated it three days after her father had died in the far north of Norway. Krogstad says he intends to show Torvald the forged loan agreement unless she gets her husband to let him stay in his position at the bank. He will keep the forged IOU to ensure that he is never dismissed. When he tells her that her forgery could send her to jail, Nora cannot believe that his blackmail will succeed. The court will surely forgive her and let her off when it is revealed that she acted out of love for her husband. Krogstad laughs at this and again advises her to confess to her husband or he will tell him himself. He leaves.

Torvald has seen Krogstad leave the house. When Nora denies that anyone has been visiting, Torvald knows she is lying. At first he is indulgent: he thinks Krogstad had begged to keep his job and Nora had pitied him. Nora has told her husband a lie, but he will forgive her, but:

> TORVALD. My little songbird must never do that again. A songbird must have a clean beak to chirp with—no false notes. (1879a, 202)

Krogstad, he tells her, is a forger and a liar. He delivers a sermon on the evils of forgery:

> TORVALD. Just think how a man like that has to wear
> a mask in the presence of those near and dear to
> him, even before his wife and children. And about
> the children, that is the most terrible part of it,
> Nora. Because such an atmosphere of lies infects
> and poisons the whole life of a house. Each breath
> that one takes in such a house is full of the breath
> of evil.

Torvald then generalizes about the culpability of the parents of such criminals:

> Nearly all cases of early corruption can be traced to
> lying mothers . . . *but of course the father's influ-*
> *ence may act in the same way.* Every lawyer is fa-
> miliar with the fact. Krogstad has been persist-
> ently poisoning his own children with lies and
> dissimulation. . . . I feel physically ill when I am
> in the company of such people. (1879a, 204–05;
> emphasis added)

The thought of her dead mother and the mention of a dishonest father affect Nora deeply. But Torvald is not aware of this and, when he finishes his condemnation, enjoins, "That is why my sweet little Nora must promise me not to plead [Krogstad's] cause." Torvald goes out, and the nurse enters and asks if she can bring in the children, who are begging to see their mother. The horrified Nora says that the nurse should not let them come to her, and then cries out to herself:

NORA. Corrupt my children? Poison my home? (*A
short pause. Then she tosses her head.*) It's not true!
It can never, never be true! (1879a, 205)

Act 1 ends with this denial—denial of both what her husband
had said about the danger of the consequences of her lying and
Krogstad's threats about the consequences of her forgery.
In act 2, Nora asks Torvald again not to dismiss Krogstad,
pretending she is afraid Krogstad will take revenge and injure
him. Torvald says that she must be thinking of her father. "Yes,"
Nora responds, "they slandered him."

TORVALD. My little Nora, between your father and
me there is all the difference in the world. Your
father's *reputation* as a public official was not
above suspicion. Mine is. (1879a, 212; emphasis
added)

Nora persists, and her husband, becoming furious, at
once writes a note dismissing Krogstad. He calls for a messen-
ger to take Krogstad the note announcing his discharge. Then
he calms down, attributing Nora's behavior to her anxiety
about him. He will forgive her for "such eloquent witness to
your great love for me" (214). She begs him to get the note
back, but it is too late.

THE PROMISE

And then Torvald, to reassure Nora that he is not afraid of
Krogstad, makes a promise that appears to justify Nora's terrible but wonderful expectation of rescue by her husband.

TORVALD. My own dear Nora, let what will happen—
when the time comes, I shall have strength and
courage enough. You shall see, my shoulders
are broad enough to bear the whole burden.
(1879a, 662)

His assertion confirms Nora's expectation of "the great thing." Torvald would take her guilt upon himself. When he leaves she is thrilled by what he has pledged, but she is also horrified and vows she will "never, never, never, never" let his sacrifice come to pass. "Anything rather than that. Anything, anything, anything!" (662).

Later she cajoles her husband into promising he will not attend to business that evening (to keep him from opening his mailbox, which now contains Krogstad's threatened revelatory letter). Torvald reluctantly agrees, calling her "my little helpless thing!" (668).

The Promised Miracle

Nora, her terror mixed with elation, expects that Torvald will inevitably read the note. She says, "After all, there's something glorious in waiting for the miracle" (670). She is contemplating suicide, yet expects that Torvald will save her somehow.

In act 3, Christine, who had known and been courted by Krogstad when they were young, persuades him to withdraw his threats. But his letter to Torvald remains in the locked box.

The Promise Renewed

Enchanted by his wife as they return from the party where she danced, Torvald rhapsodizes:

TORVALD. My darling wife! I feel as if I could never
hold you close enough. Do you know, Nora, I
often wish some danger might threaten you,
that I might risk body and soul, and *everything,*
everything for your dear sake. (675; emphasis
added)

Following this iteration of THE PROMISE (with Torvald's unknowingly using words that recall Nora's vows of "never, never"
and "anything, anything"), she

> *(tears herself from him and says, firmly)* Now you
> should read your letters, Torvald.
> [He leaves to get his mail. Nora stares wildly, throws
> her shawl over her head.]
> NORA. *(whispers hoarsely and brokenly)* Never to see
> him again. Never, never, never. Never to see the
> children again. Never, never.[17] Oh that black icy
> water! Oh, that bottomless [lake]—if it were only
> over! (1879a, 676)

But before she can run out to drown herself, Torvald comes in,
holding the letter, shouting that it can't be true. She tries to run
out but he holds her back.

> NORA. You shall not save me, Torvald. It is true.
> I have loved you beyond all else in the world. . . .

[17] The crescendo of repeated "nevers" in the last part of the play recalls
King Lear's terrible outcry of "nevers" when he realizes Cordelia, whom he is
holding in his arms, is dead. The poignant repetitions mark the unacceptable.

You shall not take my guilt upon you! (1879a,
676)

Nora then perceives that Torvald neither understands nor cares
what she is saying. He is enraged at her and afraid for himself,
with no thought of her feelings or her welfare. He has no intention of fulfilling his promise to rescue her from danger no
matter what would happen. He denounces her as

> a hypocrite, a liar—and worse, a criminal. *I* ought
> to have foreseen something of the kind. All your
> father's dishonesty—be silent! All the dishon-
> esty you have inherited—no religion, no moral-
> ity, no sense of duty. How *I* am punished for
> shielding him! *I* did it for your sake, and you re-
> ward *me* like this. You have destroyed *my* whole
> happiness. You have ruined *my* future. . . . *I*
> might even be suspected of collusion. Do you
> understand now what you have done to *me?*
> (676; emphases added)

The disenchanted Nora, even further disturbed by the attack
on her father, whose uncaring selfishness Torvald is repeating,
suddenly recognizes that her promised miracle has completely
vanished—along with the idealization of her husband. It is a
negative epiphany. She coldly and calmly answers that she does
understand.

　　Her sudden grasp of his narcissism and selfishness is then
further deepened. Krogstad returns Nora's IOU, which Torvald can now tear up. The danger of blackmail is over. Torvald
(after he has joyfully announced to her, "*I* am saved. Nora, *I*

am saved"[18] [677; emphasis added]) begins to treat the whole matter as if it had never happened. He expects to go back to the old relationship with his dear little wife, as if nothing had occurred. Besides, he now says, he realizes Nora ("my scared little songbird") did it all out of love for him.

But it is too late. Nora has taken an abrupt giant step toward separation and growing up. She no longer feels suicidal. She has, in her traumatic disillusionment, renounced THE PROMISE—her husband's and her father's promise—of rescue by what she now recognizes as a flawed, self-serving parental authority. She realizes that she has lived out a lie all her life. Nora tells Torvald that they have never had a serious talk together. She does not love him now, and he has never really loved her. "I have been your doll-wife as at home I used to be papa's doll-child."[19] She has never been happy, only merry—to amuse him. Nora has gained resolution from despair. She is determined to leave her husband and even her children—she is here repeating toward her children her mother's desertion of her. (Nora rationalizes the hurtfulness she is inflicting on them by her confidence that they will be cared for by her beloved nurse, who raised her after her mother's death.) She will walk out of her doll's house and learn how to become a woman and a real wife and mother. To remain together, she says to her husband, "the miracle of miracles would have to happen . . . Both of us would have to change—Oh, Torvald, *I no longer believe in miracles*" (681; emphasis added). And Nora walks out, the

---

[18] No "we" here.

[19] Fjelde (1978) points out that at the start of the play Nora has purchased a sword, a trumpet, and a toy horse for her two sons, but a doll and a doll's bed for her daughter, suggesting her passing the doll identity down to the next generation (121).

play ending with the sound of her slamming shut the heavy front door—a sound that has been called a late nineteenth-century knell announcing the beginning of the end of legal, if not psychological, discrimination against women.[20]

Nora's liberation and maturation can be seen as the result of her becoming aware of the continuation of her having assumed the role of plaything for her husband, a role assigned first by her father. (A psychoanalyst might say that Nora has realized the meaning of transference.) By renouncing THE PROMISE, she has achieved a partial self-analysis—a lesson learned from life rather than from therapy.

The slamming of the door should not be idealized. Nora is a fictional character, and, as with a patient who is terminating analysis, one cannot know that her future will include a happy ending. Nora would have to accept change. She still has her faults and weaknesses. Hopefully, the truth she has learned about her father, her husband, and herself would set her free enough to replace THE PROMISE of miracle by a more realistically based "promise" that she has a chance of fulfilling.[21] Of course, in contrast to a patient (where time might tell), a fictional character has no future after the end of the play.

---

[20] When a production in Germany was planned soon after *A Doll's House* was produced in Scandinavia (1879), Ibsen was forced to furnish an alternative happy ending. He never allowed this again. When the great actress Eleanora Duse wanted to do the play in Italian twelve years later, she also demanded a happy ending. Ibsen refused and in a letter to his translator noted that the German production only had had a short run; his original version of the play had subsequently been done successfully and was still being staged all over the world. He added, "I might honestly say that it was for the sake of the last scene that the whole play was written" (1891b, 301).

[21] Chekhov (1894–04): "Man will only become better when you make him see what he is like" (94).

Patient E, Nora, and Hedda Gabler

The patient I described at the beginning of this chapter was, like Nora, haunted from childhood and made vulnerable by her near-delusional expectations of promise. But E's reactions to the sense of entitled fulfillment resemble Nora's less than the reactions of another of Ibsen's heroines, Hedda Gabler. Hedda is cruel, fierce, dauntless, and determined. Hedda, unlike Nora, starts off seething with discontent with the nonfulfillment of the promise of her childhood. She also was spoiled by her father, General Gabler. In contrast to Nora, who primarily submitted to her father, Hedda has primarily identified with hers. (*Hedda Gabler* was written in 1891, twelve years after *A Doll's House*. During those years Ibsen's feelings about his wife had turned from happiness to increasing discord and bitterness.)

Hedda is unhappy in her marriage. But, unlike Nora, she knows it before the play begins. At the start of the play she feels disgusted and furious because she is aware but refuses to accept (or to inform her husband) that she is pregnant. Unlike Nora, she hates sex and does not care for children. Trapped in a marriage to a man she despises and mistreats, she ends as a suicide, identifying with her father by killing herself "heroically" with one of the general's pistols.[22]

Full Circle Back to Patient E

E had complained of depression, but there was no danger of suicide. After years of psychoanalysis, she became able to face, work on, and greatly diminish the power of THE PROMISE. She

---

[22] Hedda was wont, teasingly, to play with one of her father's brace of pistols, pointing the loaded gun at others as well as at herself.

divorced her first husband, married a caring, successful, and mildly masochistic man and had several children. I saw her in a consultation several years after the termination of her analysis.[23] She seemed to be able to enjoy her work, but—more important to her—felt she could love her second husband and, especially, her children. THE PROMISE had been reduced to life with less achievement but much satisfaction, some happiness, and a sense of considerable but not delusional promise.

Therapy

Nora has her eyes opened in a *coup de théatre*. For patients who are chronically "haunted" by parental imagos, gaining insight takes a long time and a bitter struggle. The (usually sadomasochistic) attachment to the parent who will fulfill the promise is desperately clung to. THE PROMISE and its consequences have to become clear to the patient. A great deal of repetitive analytic work by both patient and analyst is necessary in order for the power of narcissistic promise to be responsibly owned. The powerful symbiotic tie and the fear of losing it can be brought to consciousness with full emotion as it comes to life in the transference of relationships from the past onto the analyst. Working toward this goal of knowing and being able to tolerate the emotional price paid for THE PROMISE should eventually allow most of these haunted patients to choose whether or not to try to attenuate it. Weakening the emotional centrality of such ties to parents is attainable. If so, the patient can become able to feel and own the unbearable longings that the child once had toward the parent, as well as the murderous

---

[23] No follow-up is possible for the fictional live Nora or the fictional dead Hedda.

rage (that comes to new life in the analysis) that the child believed—but the adult need no longer believe—would kill the parent. If there is no attenuation, the coming to life of these feelings can now threaten to do away with the analyst the patient now feels he cannot live without. The patient may find that the intense need to hold onto becoming (identifying with) or belonging to (giving into or compulsively provoking) the parent and analyst produces transference feelings of impending loss that are too intense to endure.[24] Some patients will choose to leave the analysis and to retain the haunting inner parental presences they feel are essential to their existence. Even so, being able to be aware of the possibility of making a choice can be very helpful. Awareness, even if mostly intellectual, can supply perspective and some emotional distance; this can make life easier. And happily, some—like Nora—have become brave enough to take the risk of choosing liberation. Change need no longer primarily mean loss.

Analysts, particularly in trying to achieve a successful termination of treatment, need to understand and interpret the adhesive qualities that are a feature of the destructiveness inherent in narcissistic entitlement. Patients can first become

[24] In Ibsen's great play *The Wild Duck* (1884), we see relevant evidence of Ibsen's conflicts and his insight. Nora, Helmer, and Dr. Stockman in *An Enemy of the People* (1882) turn out to be strong enough to face reality and stand alone against convention and corruption. But Hjalmar Ekdahl in *The Wild Duck* is too weak to give up the promise associated with his illusions, and his life is shattered in his attempt to face the reality he cannot bear. In the 1884 play, Gregors Werle insists on Hjalmar facing the truth that will destroy his whole family. Werle plays the destructive truth-telling role in contrast to Dr. Stockman, who is the heroic truth-telling enemy of the people. All three men are aspects of Ibsen himself. Some ordinary people cannot live without their illusions or quasi-delusions. Eugene O'Neill echoes this observation, using the awkward word "pipedreams" in his Ibsen-like play *The Iceman Cometh* (1946).

able to know, feel fully and responsibly, and therefore to *own* the power of parental promise and their motivation to cling to it. Owning at least makes choice possible through the use of conscious will. Renunciation, or at least amelioration, of THE PROMISE and the psychic ties to parents frees up motivation toward actively achieving fulfillment of realistically possible change for the better. Then, if Fate allows, present and future life can, unlike the fettered haunting of the past, bring transcendence as well as repetition, fulfillment as well as promise.

XIV
What Do I Know?

When something ceases to be mysterious it ceases to
be of absorbing concern to scientists. Almost all the things
scientists think and dream about are mysterious.

—*Freeman Dyson,* Infinite in All Directions *(1987)*

This final chapter should perhaps be titled, as a variation on Montaigne, "What do *we* know?" I am not speaking personally but rather trying to do my inadequate best to express something about the limitations of human knowing. So much about our minds, about human nature, and about the nature of the universe seems inherently unknowable. How can we grasp infinity? How can we get beyond the limitations of our senses, of our minds, of human nature itself? Is there a God? Why is there evil in the world? Does life have a purpose? What is death? Can individual identity continue after death? These unanswerable questions are clichés. One can say, as the book of Job counsels, "Don't ask!" But it seems part of our

nature to try to comprehend all we can. Again, I am trying to
emphasize the importance of knowing how much we don't know.

A Brief Clinical Example

The clinical contact was also brief—one consultation. Patient
L, a twenty-four-year-old single woman, was seen in consultation some years ago. She lived in the South and had been told
by her psychotherapist, who had apparently read my book
about child abuse, *Soul Murder* (1989), to travel to New York
to seek advice from me. She described herself as having been
a quiet, dependent child. Her mother died when the girl was
twelve. Shortly afterward her father had requested and required that she sleep in his bed. This went on until she entered
college. She remembered no overt sexual contact, "certainly no
intercourse." What she did remember was "only cuddling for
warmth."[1] As a teenager she had "been bashful and anxious."
Her father had declared that she was too shy and thus unable
to protect herself, and he was therefore against her going out
with boys. She began to rebel against this while at college (close
to but not in her home city). There she developed close friendships with several girls and had had an occasional (usual a
single) date with a boy. (None of these boys were named or
came to individual life in her descriptions; they seemed to have
been either shy and passive or indifferent to her.) Nothing had
happened but kissing, she assured me. Her girlfriends had told
her (without knowing about her sharing the father's bed) that
she was too close to her father. She consulted a college coun-
selor, who referred her to a therapist. To L's surprise her father
consented to this, and she had now been in once-a-week ther-

---

[1] The "certainly" and the "only" (unsolicited by any questions from me
in the single consultation) made me suspect there might have been more
than "cuddling," but this could not be confirmed.

apy that her father was paying for for over two years. Several months after graduating from college and beginning a job in her hometown, she had, on the suggestion of her psychologist, moved out of her father's house. (Her therapist seemed to have taken on her father's role in telling her what to do.) She now shared an apartment with a girlfriend from college. She stated that she was now "a little less shy" and wanted to feel more independent, but she added, "*My doctor told me*[!] I am making progress in distancing my father." (I feared she was talking here as a ventriloquist's dummy.) She seemed still overwhelmingly beset by her inhibitions, anxiety, and self-deprecation. When she asked me what she should do, I felt she was expecting a magical formula that would make everything all right.

At the end of the consultative session, she asked if she could sit in my waiting room until her father came to call for her. I asked why she had come to New York with her father. "Oh," she said, "he would never let me travel without him." Here I lost some control and asked, with a tone of incredulity I was unable to suppress, if they were in the same hotel room. Yes, they were, but she reassured me they were sleeping in contiguous twin beds: "Father said he couldn't afford separate rooms." I was left with a mixed feeling of indignation and sadness—indignation at the father and sadness for both of them. It was not a surprise that L failed to show up at her scheduled second consultative appointment. I felt I knew a lot from the short contact, but there was so much that I didn't know. And, sadly, there was so much she wouldn't let herself know.

The Psychoanalytic *Weltanschauung*

What does a psychoanalyst know? Freud, like all great thinkers, certainly insisted on how much we do not and perhaps even cannot know. He also reassured us, as part of his exploration of the mind, that we know more than we think we do, reminding us of what he felt he had discovered, the existence of unconscious knowledge. (Freud *was* the definitive explorer of the unconscious mind, although he had, and knew that he had, philosophic and literary predecessors.) There are many kinds of knowing. Pascal (1660) wrote the psychologically astute maxim, "Le coeur a ses raisons que la raison ne connaît point" (The heart has its reasons that reason knows nothing of) (78). The reasons of the heart of the individual are what the patient and the psychotherapist need to attempt to discover and explore.

I hope that this book's sampling of lives that aims to show the power of resistance to change, even for the better, will convince readers that all humans are burdened with a core of unconscious functioning that remains haunted by parental ghosts. These dynamically changeable and individually variable psychic presences necessarily help form, and yet also compromise, both the sense of oneself as a separate identity and our feelings of authenticity. Authenticity consists of having arrived at possessing "enough" ability to know and own essentially (if never all the time or completely) who we are and how we feel, think, and act (and to remember responsibly how we felt, thought, and acted). The variegated phenomena involving individuals' being haunted by parental ghosts exist over wide and complex spectra that vary in quantity and intensity and that profoundly affect mental functioning. The psychic existence of these unconscious maternal and paternal (and primal parental)[2] phantoms contributes both for the better and for the worse—to strengths, achievements, and happiness as well as to weaknesses, inhibitions, and misery. These presences from the past

---

[2] "Primal parental" means the earliest mental representation consisting of an all-powerful bisexual other.

(that Freud called *revenants*) are both cause of, and enable transcendence of, psychic conflicts. It is of course true that human beings are and can remain haunted by occasions of overwhelming emotion, traumatic and ecstatic, that occur in life after early childhood, but these later hauntings are connected by unconscious fantasy with the basic earliest haunting by parents.

To repeat one of my epigraphs: Dante wrote in *The Divine Comedy*, "Nessun maggiore dolore che ricordarsi del tempo felice nella miseria" (There is no greater sorrow than to remember a time of happiness in the midst of misery) (Inferno, V, 121–24, 42; my translation). Dare we, should we, can we give up that promise of happiness that threatens to compromise our need to know in order to adapt to an inevitable tragic reality? Tragic reality is, thankfully, not the whole existential emotional truth about our existence, but in order to tolerate the human condition we have to know, with bitterness or with resignation, that change, also and eventually ultimately, means loss. The loss or at least attenuation of power of the haunting bad parental *revenants* (that threaten to take us back to or make us stick to the past of our childhood) is accomplished only if the patient first gets to know and accept that they are there. That crucial first step means becoming capable of facing the loss of the magical promise of the earliest times of life, a promise inherent to narcissism. (To fear death and Hell less, we must either delusionally insist on or renounce the promise of Heaven.) The patient must get to know and care about the price that is paid for holding onto the dependence of childhood—a dependence that can rob the present and the future of meaning. Renunciation of the false promise of, and the feeling of entitlement to, paradise must be felt in the perspective of our relation to the parents of the past. Their unconscious presences have become part of our mental structure, where they can function as ghosts, good as well as bad, who can take over without our conscious awareness.

For the psychotherapist to accomplish meaningful change in the structure and functioning of the mind—change in the direction of attaining independence, separate identity, and authenticity—the parents who haunt the mind have to be exorcised. Yet the loss of their power and their promise can only and should only be partially accomplished. Even modification (and therefore diminution of power and promise) can be achieved in some patients only after a fierce resistance to analytic treatment that involves a battle within the patient's mind, the details of which must become responsibly known and *owned*. He or she must become willing to know and to care about and finally to own their burden of being haunted by parents. The will to do so arises out of love (the *caritas* of the Bible) for the analyst—love that must also first be felt and known, love that can be held in the mind to balance out the inevitable hate.[3] Retaining love toward the analyst has to be renounced and eventually (during and after the end of the analysis) diminished. And psychological therapists must be able to know about and to empathize with this haunting. The patients must be able to *tolerate* the loss of what I have, quoting my patient, been calling (in her reverent, emphatic tone which poignantly expressed the entranced child's idealization) THE PROMISE.[4]

The promise of positive change can result in health as well

---

[3] Betty Joseph (1986) writes of the infant's need optimally to achieve being "able to bear both his love and his hate at the same time and towards the same person" (194). This achievement needs to be restored to resistant patients.

[4] The tone evoked the emotions and imagery of the child's wonder and glory in Wordsworth's "Ode to Immortality" and in his autobiographical poem, "The Prelude" (see chapter 4).

as pathology. The child's wonderful expectations of the parents (repeated in relation to the analyst) can, if individuation is achieved, lead to influencing the individual's own ambitions and accomplishments in predominantly positive ways. But delusional promise that had been needed to distance the knowledge of the hate-filled, terrible expectations of change needs to be modified and renounced, or else a malignant haunting can continue. The achievement of change in psychoanalytic treatment depends on the patient and analyst becoming able to get the patient to allow the emotions of the past that have come to full life in relation to the analyst in the course of the treatment to connect the past and present feelings. The linking of the intense past feelings that have been transferred onto the analyst in the present do not reproduce what actually happened in the past. What is revived are the reactions to, and the mind's representations of, the events and the fantasies of the past.

There is a current widespread oversimplification (by individuals and in the press) of ascribing psychic pathology almost *entirely* to dramatic traumata like child abuse.[5] This reductive formula ignores both the complexity and unpredictability of the consequences of human experiences and the effects of chronic and subtle traumatic circumstances. Actual child abuse and deprivation do, I believe, have predominantly destructive scarring effects on subsequent development. But what the reductive simplifications disregard, above all, are the complicated, often distorted, but potent fantasies that arise in relation both to what has actually happened and to what has previously been fantasized about the past. Memories and fantasies may have distorted "what has really happened" (to quote patient P,

---

[5] There are also many who ignore or deny the effects or even the occurrence of child abuse.

described below).[6] But fantasies as well as memories make up the mental registrations from the past that continue to be present, again with distorting changes, in subsequent development. It is the current version of these (I am emphasizing the registrations of the parents of the past) that can become conscious with relative certainty in the present as they focus on the analyst.

One patient, P, returned to see me years after a long treatment that was largely preoccupied by his ruminations about whether or not he had been sodomized by his father.[7] Both of us felt that he had neither established nor ruled out in his analysis that the sexual events had actually happened. The patient seemed to have reached a stalemate because of his stubborn, resistant need to minimize his feelings toward me. "I can't face feeling those things toward you," he said. The treatment ended rather suddenly when he had to go live in another country in order to keep his job. I was not sure that I had helped him and suggested he continue analysis there with someone else. He did not do so, but he had returned to tell me that he wanted to express his gratitude for what he felt I had done for him and to tell me about the positive changes he had made since he had last seen me: "I may never be able to be certain what my father did to me sexually. But I have the perspective that it might have happened. And at least I can know and actually feel what went on between us in relation to what I remember with certainty—the undeniably bad, as well as some good, nonsexual things that did occur."

---

[6] We can know with certainty that there was a Holocaust; but the individual memories of concentration camp survivors can be larded with distortions. The listener or observer can never know for certain—e.g., the "Rashomon" phenomena.

[7] The ruminations served the patient as resistances to exploring the memories of chronic mistreatment by his father that he was certain about.

I felt that in my absence he had been able to integrate much that had been brought up in the analysis, that this had brought him some perspective that connected past with present, and that he had done his best to own what was there in his mind about the past. His self-esteem and sense of identity seem to have been augmented.

Those Who Are Not Patients

We all (in varying degrees of intensity) have been, or have the fantasy that we have been, subject as children to deprivation and abuse at the hands of parents. This conviction is inevitable (although usually not in responsible consciousness); it is an inevitable consequence of our genetic heritage and what happens in the course of a development that requires a prolonged period of dependency on parents and physical care by parental figures. Even the best of parents can never fulfill the promise of keeping us from pain and frustration, hurt, and death. Parents are not gods, but our need for them to be so keeps them in our minds as powerful motivational psychic presences (for better and for worse) that can come to full life in situations of need, danger, and loss. Some of us remain more haunted than others.

Achieving Change

It follows that the topics I have dealt with can apply to anyone—not only those who are, have been, or might be anticipating psychoanalytic treatment (therapy or analysis). The advantageous power of psychoanalysis is that, if effective, it can bring the past, and especially the parents of the past, to life in the present. The emotional reexperience can make for knowing, resulting in making it easier to own.[8] Exploring one's memory, seeing, understanding, and fighting past the resistances to that exploration, and trying to establish the degrees of doubt and certainty about what did or didn't happen in the past are all *active* processes. The activity enhances self-esteem by counteracting the predominantly passive, sadomasochistic bonds to the parental imagoes—the bonds that prolong the subjection and rebellion of the past. Active fighting pushes away the paralyzing wish to wait passively for the fulfillment of the delusional false magic promise of the parents' change to benevolent gods who will undo everything bad and transform it to everything good—to Paradise regained.

And for others not motivated for treatment yet still consciously wanting change for the better, an awareness of the influence of the past and the possible effect (good as well as evil) of being haunted by parents can still be useful. This category includes those afflicted with bad expectations and insistence on the promise of magical rescue, with compulsive and maladaptive actions and insistent bad feelings, moods, and symptoms: repetitive anxieties and fears that may not be justified by the realities of the present. Such people are also driven by the need to fail and to avoid or reverse pleasure and accomplishment. One can, if motivated, become able to use conscious will to explore and ask oneself seriously about the nature and consequences of one's thought, feelings, and actions. The relevant

---

[8]It is important to remember that what comes to life and consciousness is a revival of what had been currently registered in the mind (consciously and unconsciously) not necessarily the "true" memories of what happened in the past (see Shengold 1999). The emotional intensities attached to those fantasies have to be brought to responsible consciousness and owned. This involves getting to know what we don't want to be there, and to have been there, in the emotions and emotional conflicts that are part of our identity.

question might be phrased as follows: "How do mother and father from childhood figure in what is wrong with me now?"[9]

I finish with a cliché: If increase in self-reflection and toleration of change and loss of the parents within the mind can be achieved by patients in therapy and then applied to their lives and by nonpatients in the course of their life development, knowledge can become power.

[9] A man who left without seeming to have responded much to analysis reported on a visit some years later that he had found himself able to profit when he discovered he could use self-reflection and ask himself meaningfully when in trouble: "Where is mother in this?" He said he could sometimes "locate mother's place in my mind, and sometimes I *am* her."

Postscript: Two Relevant Quotations

My penultimate quotation is from William Faulkner's *Light in August*. It needs an introductory explanation.

Joe Christmas, a foundling, black but light enough to pass for white, has been brought up in an orphanage for white children where he is shunned and stigmatized as a "nigger" by the other children. He is emotionally neglected and traumatized by the adult caretakers and persecuted specifically by a psychotic woman dietitian.[1] When adopted, at five, he is and continues to be beaten regularly by his cruel, stern, religiously obsessed foster father. His adoptive mother loves and pities him but is too weak and intimidated to protect him from her husband's wrath. She wants to be kind and surreptitiously tries to tend to and comfort him. The boy rejects and hates her and

---

[1] The five year old had been excited and terrified by witnessing the sexual intercourse of the orphanage dietitian and one of the doctors there. The woman discovers the boy hiding behind a screen, realizes she had been seen, and fears he will tell and get her fired. She becomes obsessed with hatred and fear of the boy and tries to have him sent to an orphanage for black children.

longs for his stern, demanding, and fanatically religious "father" whose frozen emotional stance he identifies with. At seventeen, his thinking is described:

> It was not the hard work which he hated, nor the punishment and injustice. He was used to that before he ever saw either of them. *He expected no less,* and so he was neither outraged nor surprised. It was the woman: that soft kindness which he believed himself doomed to be forever victim of and which he hated worse than he did the hard and ruthless justice of men. *"She is trying to make me cry,"* he thought, lying cold and rigid in his bed. . . . "She was trying to make me cry. Then she thinks that they would have had me" (1932, 147; emphasis added).

To cry and to feel love would have opened him up emotionally to reexperience the cruelty and torment of the family concentration camp that only his emotional hardening (augmented by mirroring his foster father) has allowed him to survive.

Joe is, and remains as an adult, haunted by parents—the ones who abandoned him and the ones who adopted him. He is haunted by the bad expectations from his past ("He expected no less") associated with them. He blames the mother figure and hates all women. Murderous hatred repeatedly breaks through his zombie-like defensive barrier. He finds himself holding a razor or a knife in the presence of people around him. He has had a long clandestine sexual affair with an older white woman. When she becomes menopausal and no longer craves his body, she rejects him. He had partly suspended the bad expectations that had protected him and opened up to her emotionally. Their sex had been an exciting sadomasochistic game he could play at and enjoy. But he cannot take the rejection and finally kills her.

. . .

My last quotation comes from one of Charles Dickens's Christmas stories, "The Haunted Man" (1848).

No mother's self-denying love, no father's counsel aided me. A stranger came into my father's place when I was but a child, and I was easily an alien from my mother's heart. My parents, at the best, were of that sort whose care soon ends, and whose duty is soon done; who cast their offspring off early, as birds do theirs; and if they do well, claim the merits, and, if ill, the pity. . . . I hear within me a Sorrow and a Wrong. *Thus I prey upon myself.* Thus memory is my curse; and, if I could forget my sorrow and my wrong, I would (243–45; emphasis added). [2]

[2] The story gets its name from Dickens's repeatedly telling the reader something that is said about the unhappy protagonist: "Everyone said he looked like a haunted man" (1848, 221). What I emphasize shows the Haunted Man's masochistic response to parental emotional neglect and lack of empathy; it reflects a distortion of something Dickens felt about his own parents.

Appendix:
Hartmann on the Genetic Point
of View and Object Constancy

The childhood shows the man
As morning shows the day.
—*Milton,* Paradise Regained *(1674)*

In my beginning is my end.
—*T. S. Eliot,* East Coker

Freud originally formulated three metapsychological points of view that he called the dynamic, the topographical, and the economic.[1] Rapaport and Gill, in their authoritative paper of 1959, added two more, largely based on earlier papers by Hartmann (1944) and by Hartmann

---

[1] These are different ways to look at the mind's activities, structure, and origins.

and Kris (1945): the adaptive and the genetic. Hartmann (1944) had stated in the course of describing his concept that certain of the mind's functions were not based on inner mental conflicts: "This view . . . certainly does not imply any neglect of the genetic point of view, which is fundamental in psychoanalysis" (35). Freud (1913) had previously written that psychoanalysis "from the very first . . . was directed towards tracing developmental processes" and had called it "a genetic psychology" (182–83).

Rapaport and Gill (1959) wrote, "Freud apparently took [the existence of psychoanalysis based on the importance of psychic beginnings] so much for granted that he saw no necessity to formulate a genetic point of view of metapsychology" (797)[2] Here is Rapaport and Gill's (1959) definition: "The genetic point of view demands that the psychoanalytic explanation of any psychological phenomenon include propositions concerning its psychological origin and development" (804). The genetic point of view then connects the past with the present, which is what we try to get the patient to do in psychoanalysis.[3] We assume that we must explore in the direction implied by the following questions: where did a psychological event originate? and how has it developed? There is also the assumption, borrowed from physiology and embryology, that the earliest events tend to have more extensive consequences than later ones and, even while subject to what Abrams (1977)

---

[2] I will cite another example from Freud—here from "Civilization and its discontents" (1930). Freud has been writing about "oceanic" and religious feelings: "One is justified in attempting to find a psychoanalytic—*that is, a genetic*—explanation of such a feeling" (65; emphasis added).

[3] And also, for the neurotic part of our minds, connects them with the future—as projected past—e.g., the "there is no life without mother" from childhood becomes the program for the future.

calls "transformations," can remain latently active.[4] The genetic point of view involves psychic functions (affects, thought, drives, defenses, danger situations, etc.) and structures (ego, id, super-ego). I am in this appendix emphasizing the genetic view of the child's relationships with others ("object relationships" in "psychoanalese") and the sense of a separate identity.[5] I think Hartmann alluded to this aspect of development in his 1945 paper (written with Kris) on the genetic approach when he writes of "the proposition . . . concerning the influences of earliest relationships on the survival and development of the child" (27). Hartmann's proposition leads to the understanding of the clinically significant widespread delusion or near-delusion persisting in the adult that "there is no life without mother."[6] The delusion derives from a powerful remnant of what was present at, or closely following, the beginning of mental life.

"Is There Life Without Mother?"

"Mother," in the question "Is there life without mother?," a quotation from a patient that epitomizes the psychological burden of those determinedly resistant to change, should not be taken literally. Sometimes it is the actual father or another mothering person who has, in the course of development after birth, taken over the primary position among the patient's intrapsychic (internalized) parent-figures. (My patients Y and Z, for

---

[4] Karl Abraham, somewhere in his papers, pointed out the analogic difference in the consequences of a pin being stuck into a child (minor) and into an embryo (catastrophic).

[5] This means acquiring the ability to feel "I love-and-hate mother and am no longer part of her."

[6] The extent and qualities of this delusion vary from individual to individual.

example, both seemed more consciously preoccupied with their fathers than with their mothers even in their [remembered] earliest years.)[7] The genetic point of view implies that the earliest forms of the parent-child line of development, from merger to separate (or relatively separate) identity, continue to exist in psychic registration, alongside and beneath current ones.[8] Unconscious methods of registration, structuring, and functioning of these figures continue on into adult life. There is psychic dynamism at work here, both regression and progression. This leads to the concept of object constancy.

Object Constancy

Heinz Hartmann (1952) coined the term "object constancy," designating the developing child's acquisition of the ability to hold the image of the mother in the mind even in her absence. He describes it as a developmental achievement leading to awareness of, and caring about, the existence of others.[9] He writes, "There is a long way from the object[10] that exists only as long as it is there to satisfy a need to the form of object relations that includes object constancy" (15).

In a 1952 paper, Anna Freud adopts Hartmann's term "object constancy." She sees him as portraying two stages in the development of relating to others: (1) relationship to the

[7] Many variations are possible, but it is my impression that the father usually becomes important and sometimes predominant after the first few years of life for most girls and boys; alongside new registrations the mother as principal primal parent still continues to exist in the unconscious mind.

[8] In latent (unconscious) form.

[9] This is *Caritas*—the biblical nonsexual love, an empathic caring about others.

[10] "Object" here is psychoanalytic jargon for the other that one relates to.

need-satisfying object (mother as need-fulfiller) and (2) object constancy.[11]

Anna Freud's Views

Anna Freud continued to use the term "object constancy" in her subsequent writings. She saw Hartmann's stages as complementary to, and capable of being merged with, two stages in the development of relations with others that had been proposed by Willy Hoffer and by Melanie Klein. Hoffer speaks of stage one as that in which the earliest "other" belonging to the external world (the primal parent) is treated by the infant as part of its own inner world (*milieu interne*) and therefore part of its self. The second stage has the other as a true psychological object that is the mental representation of a parental someone whose existence outside the child's mind and body can be assumed and consciously acknowledged. Klein writes of two stages of (1) part-object relationship (e.g., the object is the breast) developing into (2) whole object relationship (the object is the mother).[12] Anna Freud (1952) agrees with all three but has her own theoretical ideas, based, like Hartmann's explanation, on the concept of psychic energy: "My views on the subject lean toward a quantitative explanation—the idea that the step from the first to the second stage, from the *milieu interne*

[11] Hartmann felt that the transition to the stage of object constancy could be explained by his modification of the psychoanalytic theory of psychic energy—the developmental change from instinct-driven energy to a neutral energy. "Neutral" means that part of the energy available to the mind becomes more modulated and less controlled by inborn and initially insistent drives like sexuality and aggression.

[12] "Part-object" is psychoanalytic jargon for that which is realistically a part of the mother's body (e.g., the breast) that is sought out to fulfill bodily and instinctual needs.

to the psychological object (Hoffer), from the need-satisfying object to object constancy (Hartmann), from part object to whole object (Melanie Klein) is determined by a decrease in the urgency of the drives themselves" (233).[13]

With maturation and development, then, the ego gets stronger and the instinctual drives (sex, aggression) get weaker. The optimal development of the controlling function (= the ego) begins to weaken the power of the motivational forces that need to be controlled (= the id).

Solnit's View

Solnit (1982) has supplied one of the best definitions of object constancy: "That state of object relations in which the child has attained the capacity to retain the memory of, and emotional tie to, parents—his primary love objects—and to feel their nurturing, guiding presence even when they are a source of frustration or disappointment or when they are absent" (202). At first glance this definition seems idealized. The object constancy of everyday life, for those past early childhood, is less than is promised by the definition. The inner reassurance that comes with the assumption that we have or have had caring parents who are registered in our mind is not and can never be a continual presence. It comes and goes, waxes and wanes, like one's ability to love, of which it is a precondition. Object constancy is subject to regression under stress, and for some, like my patients X, Y, and Z, regresses too easily. But owing to the vicissitudes of fortune in life, even the most secure adult can sometimes feel like a motherless child a long way from

---

[13] Hartmann would have called this an increase in neutralization of the drives.

home (and garden) and be transiently convinced that there is no life without mother. As Solnit wisely writes, "Object constancy may never be achieved or, even if achieved, could be lost in children who suffer from repeated or prolonged periods of emotional deprivation" (205).

I would say, and I am sure Solnit would have agreed, that the attainment of object constancy is also interfered with by prolonged periods of traumatic usage, of overstimulation and torment, of chaotic and hostile parenting. (It is implicit that bad parenting of any repetitive or chronic nature also means the concomitant *deprivation* of loving, caring, empathic emotion.)

In a panel discussion in 1968 at the International Psycho-Analytical Congress, Anna Freud described the achievement of object constancy as meaning being "tied to [the parent] good or bad, for better or worse." I have been describing people who, motivated by need, feel tied to the parent, bad and worse, driven by the delusional expectation of a magical transformation to good and better. What is delusional here results from the compulsion to hold on to the (false) promise that the next contact with the parent will bring pleasure and gain and NOT loss. The urgent need not to lose the actual and/or psychically internalized parent dictates that learning how to tolerate and how to deal with the patient's murderous rage as it focuses on the analyst, whom the patient longs to love, can present the hardest task for both patient and analyst. The patient has a most difficult task. He or she must overcome the resistance to a dangerous tolerance that threatens loss by becoming able to bear both the love and the hatred in responsible consciousness at the same time.

References

Abrams, S. 1977. The genetic point of view: antecedents and transformations. *J. Psychoanal. Assn.* 25, 417–25.

Adamson, J. 2001. *Love Letters: Leonard Woolf and Virginia Ritchie Parsons. 1941–1968.* London: Chatto and Windus.

Aksakov, S. 1852. *Notes of a Provincial Wildfowler.* Translated by K. Windle. Evanston: Northwestern Univ. Press, 1998.

———. 1856a. *A Russian Gentleman.* Oxford: Oxford Univ. Press., 1994.

———. 1856b. *A Russian Schoolboy.* London: Oxford Univ. Press, 1974.

———. 1858. *Years of Childhood.* London: Edward Arnold, 1916.

Arnold, M. 1849. The Forsaken Merman. In *Poems of Matthew Arnold.* Oxford: Oxford Univ. Press, 1913, 80–83.

———. 1867. Dover Beach. In *The New Oxford Book of English Verse,* edited by H. Gardner, 703. Oxford: Oxford Univ. Press, 1972.

Auden, W. H. 1940. In memory of Sigmund Freud (died September 1939). In *The Oxford Book of American Verse,* edited by F. O. Matthiessen, 1047–51. New York: Oxford Univ. Press, 1950.

———, and Louis Kronenberger. 1962. *A Book of Aphorisms.* New York: Viking.

Bayley, J. 1974. Introduction to S. Aksakov (1856). *A Russian Schoolboy.* Oxford Univ. Press, 1974.

Chaucer, G. 1385?. *The Canterbury Tales.* In *Chaucer's Poetry,* edited by E. T. Donaldson. New York: Ronald Press, 1958.

Chekhov, A. 1892–1904. *Notebooks of Anton Chekhov,* translated by S. S. Koteliansky and L. Woolf. New York: Ecco Press, 1987.

———. 1892–1904. *Notebooks.* New York: Dover, nd.

Cheney, A. 1975. *Millay in Greenwich Village.* University: Univ. of Alabama Press.

Christy, R. , comp. 1888. *Proverbs, Maxims and Phrases of All Ages.* New York: G. P. Putnam's.

Coates, I. 1998. *Who's Afraid of Leonard Woolf?* New York: Soho Press, 2000.

Crankshaw, E. 1982. Introduction to *A Russian Gentleman* by Sergei Aksakov. Oxford: Oxford Univ. Press, 1916.

Dante. 1300?. Inferno. In *La Divina Commedia,* edited by G. Vandelli. Milan: Ulrico Hoelpli, 1928.

Denham, J. 1655. Of prudence. In *Hoyt's New Cyclopedia of Practical Quotations,* edited by K. Roberts. New York: Funk and Wagnalls, 1923, 922.

Dickens, C. 1848. The haunted man. In *A Christmas Carol and Other Stories.* New York: Modern Library, 1995, 219–31.

Durkin, Andrew. 1983. *Sergei Aksakov and Russian Pastoral.* New Brunswick: Rutgers Univ. Press.

Dyson, F. 1988. *Infinite in All Directions.* New York: Harper and Row.

Eliot, T. S. 1922. The waste land. In *American Poetry. The 20th Century.* Volume 1. New York: Library of America, 2000, 744–60.

Epstein, D. 2001. *What Lips My Lips Have Kissed: The Loves and Love Poems of Edna St. Vincent Millay.* New York: Henry Holt.

Faulkner, W. 1932. *Light in August.* New York: Modern Library, nd.

Feldman, M. 1993. The dynamics of reassurance. *Inter. J. Psychoanal.* 74: 275–86.

Fjelde, R. 1978. *Ibsen: The Complete Major Prose Plays.* New York: New American Library.

Fliess, R. 1956. *Erogeneity and Libido.* New York: International Univ. Press.

Forster, E. M. 1927. *Aspects of the Novel.* New York: Harcourt and Brace.

Fraser, R. 1988. *The Brontës: Charlotte Brontë and Her Family.* New York: Ballantine Books, 1990.

Freud, A. 1952. The mutual influences of the development of ego and id. In *The Writings of Anna Freud,* IV: 230–44. New York: International Univ. Press.

———. 1968. Panel Discussion. *Inter. J. Psychoanal.* 49: 506–12.

Freud, S. 1900. The interpretation of dreams. *SE* 5,6.

———. 1909. Notes upon a case of obsessional neurosis. *SE* 10: 153–318.

———. 1913. Totem and tabu. *SE* 13: 1–154.

———. 1916. On transience. *SE* 14: 305–07.

———. 1917. A childhood recollection from *Dichtung und Wahrheit. SE* 17: 145–66.

———. 1919. A child is being beaten. *SE* 17: 177–204.

———. 1920. Beyond the pleasure principle. *SE* 18: 7–66.

———. 1923. The ego and the id. *SE* 9: 3–68.

———. 1937. Analysis, terminable and interminable. *SE* 23: 211–25.

————. 1940. An outline of psycho-analysis. *SE* 23: 144–208

————. 1941. Findings, ideas, problems. *SE:* 23: 299–300.

Genesis. In *The Torah. The Five Books of Moses.* Philadelphia: Jewish Publishing Society of America, 1962, 1–96.

Gill, S. 1989. *William Wordsworth, A Life.* Cambridge: Oxford Univ. Press.

Gurney, D. 1913. The Lord God planted a garden. In *The Home Book of Modern Verse,* edited by B. Stevenson, 336–37. New York: Henry Holt, 1925.

Haggard, H. R. *She.* New York: Grosset and Dunlap, 1926.

Hamilton, E. 1940. *Mythology.* London: Penguin.

Handel, G. 1742. *The Messiah.* New York: Scribner's, nd.

Hartmann, H. 1944. Psychoanalysis and sociology. In *Essays on Ego Psychology.* New York: International Univ. Press, 1964.

Hartmann, H. 1952. The mutual influences in the development of ego and id. *Psychoanal. Study Child* 7: 9–30.

————, and E. Kris 1945. The genetic approach to psychoanalysis. *Psychoanal. Study Child* 1:11–30.

Heine, H. 1830? The picture gallery. In *Self-Portrait and Other Prose Writings,* edited by F. Ewen, 128. Secaucus, N.J.: Citadel Press, 1948.

Homeric Hymn. c. 800–600BC?. The snatching of Persephone. In *The Penguin Book of Greek Verse,* edited and translated by C. A. Tryponis, 118–19. Baltimore: Penguin Books, 1971.

Housman, A. E. 1922. Poem xii. In *Last Poems.* London: Richards Press.

Ibsen, H. 1879a. A doll's house. In *Eleven Plays of Henrik Ibsen.* Volume 2. New York: Modern Library, nd, 175–254.

————. 1879b. A doll's house. In *World Drama,* edited by B. Clarke, translated by W. Archer, 642–81. Dover Publications, 1933.

————. 1891. Hedda Gabler. In *Eleven Plays Of Henrik Ibsen.* Volume 1. New York: Modern Library, nd, 205–305.

————. 1896. John Gabriel Borkman. In *Works of Henrik Ibsen,* translated by W. Archer. New York: Himbaugh and Brown, 1911.

Johnstone, K. 1998. *The Hidden Wordsworth.* New York: W. W. Norton, 2002.

Joseph, B. 1986. Psychic change and the psychoanalytic process. In *Psychic Equilibrium and Psychic Change. Selected Papers of Betty Joseph* edited by M. Feldman and E. Bott Spillius, 192–202. London: Routledge, 1989.

Kaye, J. 1993. *The Life of Benjamin Spock.* New York: Henry Holt.

Keats, J. 1819. Letter to G. and T. Keats of 21 December 1819. In *Letters of John Keats.*

Kipling, R. 1937. Something of myself. In *Complete Works of Rudyard Kipling.* Volume 24: 349–518. New York: Doubleday and Doran, 1941.

Levi, P. 1987. *The Drowned and the Saved.* London: Abacus, 1990.

Lukashevich, S. 1965. *Ivan Aksakov 1823–1886*. Cambridge: Harvard Univ. Press.

Maier, T. 1998. *Dr. Spock: An American Life*. New York: Harcourt Brace.

Marcus, S. 1992. A case history before Freud: Intimations of the unconscious in Wordsworth. In *Explorations: The Nineteenth Century*. Lafayette, La.: The Levy USL Press.

Marvell, A. 1681. The Garden. In *Marvell*, edited by J. Summers, 102–04. New York: Dell, 1961.

Millay, E. 1912. Renascence. In *The Selected Poetry of Edna St. Vincent Millay*, edited by N. Milford. New York: Modern Library, 2002.

———. 1920. First fig. In *Collected Lyrics of Edna Vincent Millay*. New York: Harper, nd, 127.

———. 1923. Scrub. In *Collected Lyrics of Edna St. Vincent Millay*. New York: Harper, nd. 160.

———. 1952. *Letters of Edna St. Vincent Millay*. Edited by A. Macdougall. New York: Grosset and Dunlap.

Milford, N. 2001. *Savage Beauty: The Life of Edna St. Vincent Millay*. New York: Random House.

Montaigne, M. 1580. *Montaigne's Essays*. Translated by Charles Cotton; edited by W. C. Hazlitt. London: A. L. Burt, 1892.

Orwell, G. 1948. *Nineteen Eighty-Four*. New York: Harcourt and Brace, 1949.

The Oxford Companion to Gardens. 1986. Edited by G. Jellicoe, S. Jellicoe, P. Goode, M. Lancaster. New York: Oxford Univ. Press.

Ozick, C. 1984. Mrs. Virginia Woolf: A madwoman and her nurse. In *Art and Ardor: Essays*. New York: E. P. Dutton.

Pascal, B. 1660. *Pensées*. London: J. M. Dent and Sons, 1931.

Rapaport, D., and M. Gill. 1959. The points of view and assumptions of metapsychology. In *The Collected Papers of David Rapaport*, edited by M. Gill, 795–811. New York: Basic Books, 1967.

Roberts, K., ed. 1922. *Hoyt's New Cyclopedia of Practical Quotations*. New York: Funk and Wagnalls.

Rodman, F. R. 2003. *Winnicott: Life and Work*. Cambridge, Perseus.

Rosenfeld, N. 2000. *Outsiders Together: Virginia and Leonard Woolf*. Princeton: Princeton Univ. Press.

Sacks, O. 2001. *Uncle Tungsten*. New York: Vintage.

Salaman, E. 1973. *The Great Confession*. London: Allen Lane.

Shakespeare, W. 1593? Sonnet 18. In *Complete Plays and Poems of William Shakespeare*. Boston: Houghton Mifflin, 1941, 1374.

———. 1596. *The Merchant of Venice*. In *The Oxford Shakespeare*. New York: Oxford Univ. Press, nd.

———. 1599. *Romeo and Juliet.* Edited by R. Hasley. New Haven: Yale Univ. Press, 1965.

———. 1600a. *The Second Part of Henry the Fourth.* New Haven: Yale Univ. Press, 1965.

———. 1600b. *The Life of King Henry the Fifth.* New Haven: Yale Univ. Press, 1965.

———. 1601. *Hamlet.* New Haven: Yale Univ. Press, 1965.

Shelley, P. 1819. Ode to the west wind. In *The Viking Book of Poetry of the English-speaking World,* edited by R. Aldington, 748–52. New York: Viking, 1941.

Shengold, L. 1989. *Soul Murder.* New Haven: Yale Univ. Press.

———. 1995. *Delusions of Everyday Life.* New Haven: Yale Univ. Press.

———. 2000. *"Is There Life Without Mother?"* Hillsdale, N.J.: Analytic Press.

Solnit, A. 1982. Developmental perspectives on self and object constancy. *Psychoanal. Study Child* 37: 201–218.

Spater, G., and E. Parsons. 1977. *A Marriage of True Minds.* New York: Harcourt, Brace, Jovanovich.

Spock, B. 1957. *Baby and Child Care.* Revised ed. New York: Pocket Books.

———. 1995. *A Better World for Our Children.* Bethesda, Md.: National Press Books.

———, and M. Morgan. 1985. *Spock on Spock: A Memory of Growing Up with the Century.* New York: Pantheon.

Spotts, F. (1989). Preface and commentary to *Letters of Leonard Woolf.* Edited by F. Spotts. New York: Harcourt, Brace, Jovanovich, 1989, ix–xiv and *passim.*

Summers, J. 1961. Introduction. In *Marvell,* edited by J. Summers, 7–26. New York: Dell, 1961.

Swinburne, A. 1860?. The garden of Proserpine and A forsaken garden. In *The New Oxford Book of English Verse,* edited by H. Gardner, 745–47, 753–55. Oxford: Oxford Univ. Press, 1972.

Tennyson, A. 1889. Demeter and Persephone. In *The Poems and Plays of Alfred Lord Tennyson.* New York, Modern Library, 1938, 844–47.

Trilling, L. 1940. Freud and literature. In *The Liberal Imagination.* New York: Viking, 1950, 34–57.

———. 1948. The Princess Casamassima. In *The Liberal Imagination: Essays on Literature and Society.* New York: Doubleday Anchor, 1950, 55–88.

———. 1950. Wordsworth and the rabbis. In *The Moral Obligation to be Intelligent: Selected Essays,* edited by L. Wiseltier, 178–202. New York: Farrar, Straus, Giroux, 2000.

Upper Rhenish Master. 1410. Painting in the Stadelsches Kunstinstitut,

Frankfurt-am-Main. Illustrated in *Art of the Late Middle Ages* by Hans Hofstatter. New York: Harry N. Abrams, 1968.

Weil, S. Quoted in W. H. Auden and Louis Kronenberger. 1962. *The Viking Book of Aphorisms.* New York: Viking, 90.

Whitman, W. 1855a. *Leaves of Grass.* New York: Modern Library, nd.

———. 1855b. *Leaves of Grass* (1891–92 edition). New York: Aventure Press, 1931, 97–105.

Wilde, O. 1896. The importance of being Earnest. In *Salomé and Other Plays.* New York: Boni and Liveright, 1919, 45–135.

Woolf, L. (1901–69). *Letters of Leonard Woolf.* Edited by F. Spotts. New York: Harcourt, Brace, Jovanovich, 1989.

———. 1960. *Sowing.* London: Hogarth Press.

———. 1967. *Downhill All the Way.* London: Hogarth Press.

———. 1969. *The Journey Not The Arrival Matters.* New York: Harcourt, Brace, Jovanovich.

Wordsworth, W. 1805/1839. *The Prelude: A Parallel Text.* Edited by J. C. Maxwell. New York: Penguin, 1971.

———. 1801. The sparrow's nest. In *Wordsworth's Poetical Works.* Oxford: Oxford Univ. Press, 1923.

———. 1807. Intimations of immortality from recollections of early childhood. In *The Complete Poems of William Wordsworth,* edited by T. Hutchinson, 587–90. London: Oxford Univ. Press, 1923.

Yeats, W. B. (1914). In dreams begins responsibility. In *The Collected Poems of W. B. Yeats.* New York: Macmillan, 1946.

———. (1928). Among schoolchildren. In *The Collected Poems of W. B. Yeats.* New York: Macmillan, 1946.

Index